# The Political Economy of Oil-Exporting Countries

1. *Venezuela*
   Juan Carlos Boué

2. *Nigeria*
   Sarah Ahmad Khan

3. *Indonesia*
   Philip Barnes

# Indonesia
# The Political Economy of Energy

Philip Barnes

Published by the Oxford University Press
for the Oxford Institute for Energy Studies
1995

Oxford University Press, Walton Street, Oxford OX2 6DP
Oxford New York
Athens Auckland Bangkok Bombay
Calcutta Cape Town Dar es Salaam Delhi
Florence Hong Kong Istanbul Karachi
Kuala Lumpur Madras Madrid Melbourne
Mexico City Nairobi Paris Singapore
Taipei Tokyo Toronto
and associated companies in Berlin Ibadan

Oxford is a trade mark of Oxford University Press

British Library Cataloguing in Publication Data
available

ISBN 0-19-730016-2

Cover design by Moss, Davies, Dandy, Turner Ltd.
Typeset by Philip Armstrong
Printed by Bookcraft, Avon

# The Political Economy of Oil-Exporting Countries

Indonesia: The Political Economy of Energy is the third in a series of books on the major petroleum and gas exporting nations, most of them part of the developing world. These countries occupy a central position in the global economy given that oil, and increasingly natural gas are the energy sources most used in the world. Oil is also the most important primary commodity in international trade. At the same time, the oil-exporting country despite progress in its efforts to diversify the economy still finds that its prospects are closely bound to the future of its oil.

Books in this series incorporate research work done at the Oxford Institute for Energy Studies. Their aim is to provide a broad description of the oil and gas sectors of the country concerned, highlighting those features which give each country a physiognomy of its own. The analysis is set in the context of history, economic policy and international relations. It also seeks to identify the specific challenges that the exporting country will face in developing its wealth to the best advantage of the economy.

# CONTENTS

# TABLES

# FIGURES

# ABBREVIATIONS

| | |
|---|---|
| APEC | Asia Pacific Economic Cooperation |
| ASEAN | Association of South East Asian Nations |
| b/cd | barrels per calender day |
| bcf | billion cubic feet |
| bcm | billion cubic metres (17,800 boe/d) |
| b/d | barrels per day |
| boe | barrels of oil equivalent (5.8 million Btu, 5.7 Gigajoules) |
| boe/d | barrels of oil equivalent per day (50 toe) |
| Btu | British thermal units |
| COW | contract of work |
| EOR | enhanced oil recovery contract |
| GW | gigawatts |
| JOA | joint operating agreement |
| JOB | joint operating bodies |
| JOC | joint operating contract |
| kW | kilowatts |
| LNG | liquefied natural gas |
| LPG | liquefied petroleum gases |
| mb | million barrels |
| mt | million tonnes |
| MW | megawatts |
| NGL | natural gas liquids |
| OECD | Organization for Economic Cooperation and Development |
| OPEC | Organization of the Petroleum Exporting Countries |
| PSC | production-sharing agreement |
| scf | standard cubic feet |
| TAC | technical assistance contract |
| tce | tonnes of coal equivalent |
| tcf | trillion cubic feet |
| TEA | technical evaluation agreement |
| toe | tonnes of oil equivalent |
| tpa | tonnes per annum |

# GLOSSARY OF INDONESIAN TERMS

*ABRI*                    Indonesian armed forces

*Bakoren*                 National Energy Coordinating Board

*Bappenas*                National Development Planning Agency

*Batan*                   National Atomic Energy Board

*BPPKA*                   Foreign Contractors Management Body

*Dewan Perwakilan Rakyat*
                          House of Representatives

*Golkar*                  Government sponsored joint secretariat of
                          functional groups and the ruling political
                          party

*IGA*                     Indonesian Gas Association

*IPA*                     Indonesian Petroleum Association

*Lemigas*                 State-owned oil and gas research body

*Majelis Permusyawaratan Rakyat*
                          People's Consultative Assembly

*Migas*                   Directorate of Oil and Natural Gas
                          (Department of Mines and Energy)

*Permina / Permindo / Pertamin / Permigan*
                          Early state oil companies, now superseded

*Pertamina*               The state oil and gas company

*PGN*                     State gas utility

*PLN*                     State electricity utility

*PT Tambang Batubara*
>   Coal industry other than Bukit Asam

*PT TBBA Tambang Batubara Bukit Asam*
>   Bukit Asam coal mining project

| | |
|---|---|
| *Repelita* | Five-Year Development Plan |
| *Repelita I* | 1969/1970–1973/1974 |
| *Repelita II* | 1974/1975–1978/1979 |
| *Repelita III* | 1979/1980–1983/1984 |
| *Repelita IV* | 1984/1985–1988/1989 |
| *Repelita V* | 1989/1990–1993/1994 |
| *Repelita VI* | 1994/1995–1997/1998 |

# 1 THE GIANT FROM THE SHADOWS: THE POLITICAL AND ECONOMIC CONTEXT OF INDONESIA'S ENERGY RESOURCES

## Before Independence: The Colonial Treasure House

Indonesia is a giant of a country placed by nature in a strategic and potentially dominating position amongst the key economies of South East Asia and Australasia. With a population of some 190 million, since the break-up of the old Soviet Union Indonesia has become the fourth most populous country in the world after China, India and the United States. There are said to be over 300 different language groups and hundreds of ethnic divisions.[1] It is a young population with approximately 45 per cent under 25 years of age. By the year 2000 there should be nearly 210 million Indonesians. Over the few years to the end of the century, Indonesia will need to find the resources to support an additional 25 million people, equivalent to the entire population of Morocco or Algeria. It also means around 2.3 million entrants to the labour market each year for whom jobs will have to be found.

The country consists of an archipelago of some 17,500 islands[2] that stretch 3,200 miles from east to west, equivalent to the distance from London to Moscow. It is in an equatorial location, spanning 15 degrees above and below the equator, with the Indian Ocean flowing into the archipelago from the west and the Pacific Ocean from the east. The land is extremely fertile with rich volcanic soil and a favourable tropical climate. It is also blessed with abundant mineral deposits and a diversity of marine and other resources.

The island of Java contains the capital, Jakarta, 60 per cent of the population and the bulk of industrial activity and energy consumption. It is one of the most densely populated areas in the world. Jakarta, the country's largest city, is a sprawling, densely populated and polluted metropolis of over 8.2 million people situated on the coastal plain of north west Java. Over-population is, however, a problem mainly confined to this island and the small island of Bali. At the far western end of the archipelago is the island of Sumatra which represents some 25 per cent of Indonesia's area with just over 20 per cent of the

1

population (see map in Appendix 1 and Table 1.1). Kalimantan, which is east of Sumatra and north of Java, shares the island of Borneo with two provinces of Malaysia and with Brunei. Sulawesi, another of the main islands, is east of Kalimantan and represents 10 per cent of Indonesia's total area with some 7 per cent of its population. Irian Jaya, the Indonesian portion of New Guinea, is the most easterly part of the country and lies directly north of Australia. It is sparsely populated and primitive, containing less than 1 per cent of Indonesia's population in 22 per cent of the land mass.

The country's political and economic development has always been strongly influenced by its location astride important trade routes connecting the Middle East, India and China. It was these trade routes which first brought significant contact with other civilizations and particularly the assimilation and adaptation of Indian culture. The Portuguese and other traders followed the same routes in their search for gold and spices, bringing with them European influence and eventually a long period of colonial rule.

**Table 1.1:**   The Major Islands of Indonesia

|  | Population Million | Area 000 Km² | Oil Production 000 Barrels Per Day | Gas Reserves Million Barrels Oil Equivalent | Coal Production Million Tonnes | Hydro Electric Potential GW |
|---|---|---|---|---|---|---|
| Java | 112 | 132 | 131 | 1,563 | - | 5 |
| Sumatra | 38 | 476 | 1,039 | 3,476 | 18 | 16 |
| Sulawesi | 13 | 189 | - | 142 | - | 10 |
| Kalimantan | 9 | 539 | 198 | 3,997 | 6 | 22 |
| Bali | 3 | 6 | - | - | - | 1 |
| Irian Jaya | 2 | 422 | 25 | 78 | - | 22 |
| Others[a] | 9 | 141 | 111[b] | 6,528[b] | - | 1 |
| Total | 186 | 1,905 | 1,504 | 15,784 | 24 | 77 |

a.    Including Maluka (the Moluccas), East Timor, North Tenggara (lesser Sundas)
b.    Including Natuna

Sources: *Indonesia: Source Book*, 1993; *World Bank Development Report*, 1992; *Petroleum Report of Indonesia*, 1991/1993

After many centuries of strong Hindu and Buddhist influence and dominance, Islam was first introduced into northern Sumatra in the thirteenth century and, by the fifteenth century, was spreading throughout the islands. This culminated in the powerful Islamic Mataram dynasty in Central Java in the late sixteenth century. Approximately 85 per cent of the population are now said to be Muslim, making Indonesia the largest Islamic nation in the world. About 10 per cent of the population are counted as Christian and some 2 per cent are Hindus, notably in Bali. All the religions have a distinctly Indonesian flavour and animism also flourishes.

The Dutch conquest of what was to become the Netherlands East Indies began in the early seventeenth century and by 1799 the islands had come under the direct rule of the Netherlands. There were short spells of occupation by the French and the British but Dutch rule continued for more than 350 years.

Dutch colonial rule was harsh, even by comparison with other colonial powers of the day, and always had the basic aim of extracting as much as possible of the natural resources of the islands for the sole benefit of the Netherlands. Cash crops such as sugar, tea and coffee were grown largely in plantations at the expense of traditional rice growing and subsistence agriculture. This inflicted considerable hardship and sometimes near starvation on the peasant population. It can be said that this ruthless exploitation of Indonesia's wealth supported the industrialization of the Netherlands; it certainly made them one of the major colonial powers. The attitude of the Indonesian government to foreign interest in its oil and gas resources was moulded and continues to be influenced by this colonial exploitation.

In the period from the beginning of the twentieth century until 1940 more attention began to be paid by the Dutch to the welfare of the people and substantial numbers of young Indonesians were sent to be educated in the Netherlands. An educated elite was created that increasingly resented European rule and helped to raise national awareness. However, there were few serious efforts by the Dutch to move the population forward to political or economic responsibility.

There were some attempts to restore independence by force but by the early twentieth century these had largely been replaced by nationalist organizations which sought change and

reform through mainly political means. Amongst these move-
ments was a study club at the Bandung Institute of Technology
led by a young engineer, Sukarno. This became the Indonesian
Nationalist Party (PNI) in 1927 and Sukarno was to become
the first president of an independent Indonesia.

### 'Earth Oil': The Early Days of the Oil Industry

The first drilling for oil was undertaken in East Java by a Dutch
plantation manager in 1884, although oil from natural seepages
had been used for many centuries. Indeed, as early as 1870 the
colonial government had drawn up a list of known recurrences.
By 1885 the first commercial volumes of oil were being produced. With interest in the region's oil increasing rapidly, the
Royal Dutch Company was formed in 1890 for the production
and refining of oil. Another early company was Shell Transport
and Trading which found oil in East Borneo and set up a small
refinery in Balikpapan in 1894. By 1907 the two companies
had merged into the Royal Dutch/Shell group of companies
and by 1911 Shell's domination of the country's industry through
its operating company BIPM was completed with the purchase
of the remaining independent producers.[3] The Netherlands East
Indies had become the major supplier of 'oil for the lamps of
Asia'.

In 1907, with the official reception of the East Indies Mining
Law of 1899 into the colony by the Governor General, the first
general mining legislation was introduced. Its provisions
paralleled the contractual principles then governing concessions
in Persia. All mineral rights were invested in the colonial
government which was authorized to grant full ownership rights
to foreign companies. Oil concessions were normally valid for
40 years with a maximum government revenue entitlement of
20 per cent of net profits. The oil industry expanded rapidly
and by 1924 the number of concessions had increased to 119,
covering a total of 6,400 sq. km. Total production had also
increased to 62,000 barrels per day, of which 95 per cent was
produced by Royal Dutch.

Preference in obtaining concessions had been given to Dutch
firms and overwhelmingly to Royal Dutch in an attempt to
continue the Dutch monopoly over all the country's resources.

However, US companies had also been interested in obtaining concessions from the very early days and eventually, after threats of counter action against Dutch companies in the United States, restrictions were relaxed. Thus, Caltex and Stanvac[4] were firmly established in Indonesia as producers and refiners well before the Second World War.

Crude production had reached 170,000 b/d by 1939 and total refining capacity some 180,000 b/d.[5] Indonesia then dominated the oil industry in the Far East where over 75 per cent of the crude oil produced came from Indonesian wells. The Second World War and the Japanese occupation in subsequent years took a heavy toll. By 1946, crude production had fallen to a low point of 5.7 thousand b/d and the refineries were a shambles.

The Japanese government and military establishment had long been interested in obtaining control of Indonesian oil and other resources. Indonesia was a key element in their expansionist policies which led to full-scale war in China in the late 1930s and later with the USA and Great Britain in December 1941. Indonesian crude oil and refineries were seen as vital for the functioning of the Japanese war machine. As the war in the Far East developed, seizure of the oil fields became inevitable and the Japanese invaded the Netherlands East Indies in January 1942. They were to stay in control until 1945.

At the beginning of the war attempts were made by the Dutch to destroy most of the oil facilities to prevent them being used

**Table 1.2:** Major Oil Companies and Oil Production in Indonesia in 1940. Thousand Barrels Per Day

| Company | Region | Production | Controlling Interest |
|---------|--------|------------|----------------------|
| BPM | N.+S. Sumatra, E. Java, N.+E. Borneo, Ceram | 96.7 | Royal Dutch |
| NIAM | S. Sumatra, N.E. Sumatra | 27.4 | Colonial Govt. and BPM |
| NKPM | S. Sumatra/Palembang, E. Java | 44.4 | Stanvac |
| NPPM | Mid-Sumatra, W. Java | Neg | Socal/Texaco (Caltex) |
| NNGPM | New Guinea | Neg | 40% Royal Dutch, 40% Stanvac, 20% Caltex |

Source: O.J. Bee, *The Petroleum Resources of Indonesia*, 1982

by the Japanese invaders. As this had to be done at great speed and with inadequate means the results were not very successful. Indeed, some facilities were left untouched. By the end of March 1942, the Japanese army had taken full control of the oilfields. Several elements of the Japanese army were specialized battalions consisting entirely of oil producing and refining personnel. Not solely by coincidence, some of them had been working in Indonesia up to a few months before the invasion. The Japanese quickly got the oil flowing from abandoned wells and restored refinery operations. Through the rest of the war years they drastically exploited the existing oil reserves and refineries for their war effort with the aid of the few experienced Indonesians and Dutch prisoners. They also drilled the discovery well of the giant Minas oilfield whose location had been prepared by Caltex in late 1941.

The country's oil reserves were drastically depleted by over-exploitation and the lack of good practices. However, one benefit came from the establishment of training schools for the oil industry to make good the shortfall in skilled workers. This had the ultimately beneficial effect of enabling many Indonesians to gain experience in oilfield and refining operations which sub-sequently helped lay the foundations for the post-war national oil industry. Indeed, the motto of the present state oil and gas organization, Pertamina, was inspired by those years: 'Learn while you work, work while you learn'.

The Japanese occupation, although costly in human terms and in damage to the oil industry, had the unexpected effect of greatly stimulating and strengthening the nationalistic move-ment. The Japanese were initially welcomed as potential liberators and developers of the so-called 'co-prosperity sphere'. Although this welcome fairly soon turned into disenchantment, the Japanese encouragement of nationalism for their own ends provided the cause with a number of opportunities for its development. Nationalist leaders were freed and Bahasa Indonesia was promoted as a nationwide language. The Japanese also allowed Sukarno and others to hold positions of authority and supported their travels around the country. This enabled nationalist leaders to build up support for the independence campaign and they naturally seized the opportunity enthusi-astically. A 'home defence corps' was also formed of Indonesian volunteers. This 'army' soon became a hot-bed of nationalism and an instrument for the military fight against the Dutch.

In 1945, with defeat looming, the Japanese set up a planning committee for independence with Sukarno as chairman. Three days after the Japanese surrender, on 17 August, 1945, Sukarno and his vice-chairman, Hatta, proclaimed independence.

## Independence and the Sukarno Years

Between 1945 and 1949, Indonesia remained in a state of war as the Dutch attempted to regain control over their former colony. There was determined Indonesian resistance and, with world opinion turning against them, the Dutch finally transferred sovereignty on 27 December, 1949. On 17 August, 1950 the new Republic of Indonesia was officially proclaimed as a unitary state.[6] Sukarno, the new president, was a charismatic figure and powerful orator with enormous prestige and the potential to bring great benefits to his country. Unfortunately this was not to be.

The president's background made him vigorously opposed to any manifestations of colonialism and capitalism and he set the economy on a somewhat muddled Marxist course. He became the natural focus for the discontent and anxieties of other ex-colonial countries and was soon something of a hero of the international left and much of the third world. He was to follow a radical and highly individualist anti-colonial and anti-imperialist stance in world politics throughout his presidency. This found expression in the conference of Afro-Asian countries held in Bandung in 1955, which launched the 'non-aligned' movement. In place of the big power conflict then the focus of world attention, Sukarno put forward a theory of confrontation which was further developed at conferences and in speeches to international audiences. This confrontation was seen as one between the 'new emerging' and the 'old established forces', of which the westerners were the 'neo-colonial imperialists'. This approach to world politics was intended to replace the old imperialist–communist dichotomy or the threefold approach of the neutralists such as Yugoslavia or India.

In 1960, with the dissolution of the elected parliament and its replacement by one appointed by the president, Sukarno achieved almost absolute power. He was, however, temperamentally unsuited to move beyond the revolutionary stage to the slower and unspectacular stage of rebuilding. Certainly, towards the end of his presidency, Sukarno's posturings on the world stage had managed to alienate almost all potentially economic and politically supportive nations, including the Soviet Union and China.

The eventual realization of the need to get US political and financial support did help to act as a partial restraint on radical adventures abroad. Nonetheless, the country was led almost inevitably to the disastrous confrontation with Malaysia in 1963. By this time, supplies of foreign aid were almost exhausted and there was a huge bill outstanding for repayment of principal and interest. Exports declined under the impact of confrontation and rampant smuggling and heavy demands were made on government revenues by the armed forces.

The economy as a whole had already been deteriorating for many years. Sukarno's years of 'guided democracy' had by the time he lost power in 1966 and after two decades of independence, brought the country to near bankruptcy. It is true that he and his government had always faced an enormous task in unifying the country as well as building up the economy after many years of devastation and neglect. They also had to cope with increasingly adverse terms of trade. However, the dissipation of political energy in the pursuit of ultra-nationalistic goals, the domestic unrest, the growing strength of the communist party,[7] and an increased lack of fiscal prudence scarcely provided the right climate for improving the economy.

The old colonial economy had been characterized by very low wages and costs, high efficiency in the plantation sector, and substantial investment in mining and some tertiary activities such as trading and communications. There was also a stable currency system and an ability to adjust to changes in global economic conditions.

Just before the Second World War, Indonesia was supplying most of the world's quinine and pepper, over one-third of its rubber, one-quarter of its coconut products and one-fifth of its tea, sugar, coffee and palm oil. At independence, the country had inherited an economy that was based overwhelmingly on small-scale agriculture, although the plantation system for growing export crops such as tea, coffee, rubber, spices and palm oil was well developed. There were established petroleum and tin industries and simple manufacturing capabilities. Rubber was the leading earner of foreign exchange; even as late as 1966 petroleum accounted for only about 30 per cent of the total commodity earnings. The nationalization of all the former Dutch-owned enterprises in 1958 transferred significant means of production to the state. It marked a turning point from which there seemed to be no going back and foreign companies shied away from Indonesia. Many army officers were put in charge of running factories, estates and trading companies and this set the pattern which continues today. Some of the profits were diverted to army units and elsewhere and smuggling of export goods flourished.

Per capita income during the 1960s was less than US $70 per annum and it proved impossible to maintain self sufficiency in food. During most of the 20 years after independence, this situation remained largely unchanged. Indonesia's agricultural output was insufficient to meet domestic consumption, forcing the country to rely heavily on loans from Warsaw Pact countries. As conditions worsened, the economy and the population had to suffer inflation rates that exceeded 600 per cent per annum.

Sukarno had to balance strong groups such as the religious parties, the army and the communist party as well as the tensions between the ethnic Chinese and the indigenous people of largely Malay stock, the 'Pribumi'. Separatism amongst the many islands always remained a problem. But internal political difficulties were aggravated by economic policies which, despite their socialist and populist labels, benefited only a narrow ruling segment of society.

The bureaucratic and political dominance of Java had been a cause of tension with the other islands since colonial days. Under Sukarno, Java continued to be favoured over the other islands. This was exacerbated by Sukarno's authoritarian style and there were a number of separatist uprisings that were in part against 'Javanization' and which were bloodily suppressed. There remains today a feeling that the national development process favours Java at the expense of the rest of the country where most of the resources are situated. In the case of energy, less than 10 per cent of the oil reserves and 20 per cent of the gas reserves are on or around Java and the major commercial coal reserves are in Sumatra and Kalimantan. Java, because of its relatively cheap labour and more developed infrastructure still tends to attract most investment despite efforts by the government to move projects and people away from the island. In 1992, for example, nearly 60 per cent of all foreign investment went to Java.

After the expulsion of the Japanese, the major oil companies, Stanvac, Caltex and Shell, returned to Indonesia. The Indonesian leaders had embodied rights to the country's natural resources in Article 33 of the 1945 Constitution which stated that all resources of land and water belonged unequivocally to the people. Shell was able to resume production in Tarakan and Kalimantan as early as 1945 and 1946.

Although there were many problems, not least as a result of the bitter war for independence and civil disorders, crude oil production regained its pre-war level by 1952. Thereafter, production increased steadily to reach more than 400,000 b/d in 1960 as Caltex developed a number of major new fields in Central Sumatra. The companies had continued to operate under 'let alone' agreements signed with the Dutch colonial government in the dying days of their rule in 1948 even after independence was achieved.[8] The old colonial Mining Law of 1899 remained in force until the enactment of the Petroleum Act of 1960.

In the early post-war period, both Shell and Stanvac had tried to obtain new exploration and development areas to maintain output, but without success. Most of the onshore fields were small, needing a large number of wells to extract the oil, and a high proportion were already on secondary recovery. Caltex was in a more favourable position than the other two companies as its concession areas were still largely undeveloped. It was therefore able to launch an intensive search for oil and soon developed the giant Minas field in Central Sumatra. This, together with the Duri field which had come into production just before the war, enabled Caltex to dominate post-war production; by 1963 it was responsible for more than half of all crude output.

All the exploration and development work of the major companies during the 1950s took place in the pre-war concessions due to the ban on the granting of new concessions.[9] As a result, the level of investment remained low. Although production continued to increase through the 1950s, the reserves to production ratio deteriorated and Indonesia's share of world output declined.

During the conflict with the Dutch, three worker oil companies were founded, one each in Java, South Sumatra and North Sumatra, to provide the Indonesian forces with fuel. One of these companies, Perusahaan Tambang Minjak Negara, is considered to be the first Indonesian oil company. This company had already been formed in 1945 when the North Sumatran oilfields were transferred by the Japanese occupation army to a group of Indonesian oil workers. It was later transferred to the Indonesian army. In 1957, when the army took over the management of the former Shell fields in North Sumatra, it appointed Dr Ibnu Sutowo to establish a limited liability company to rehabilitate the oil industry and to export oil. This new company, P.T. Permina, exported its first oil from the old wells to Japan in 1958. Subsequently, Permina obtained credit and technical assistance from Japan which was used to rehabilitate the surface facilities and buy drilling rigs.[10] By 1962 an oil academy to train Indonesians had been established at Bandung, later to be transferred to Cepu.

Throughout the 1950s, Shell and Stanvac had negotiated for additional exploration and development areas adjacent to their main producing fields in order to maintain and increase crude production. The negotiations were not successful. On the other hand the government, starting in 1959, undertook a number of individual contracts with foreign companies other than Shell, Caltex and Stanvac. This was probably to demonstrate their independence in oil matters and soften up the majors for new demands.

The freeze on new concessions lasted until 1960 when the Oil and Mining Law No. 44 was brought in. This Law established the principle that 'all extraction of petroleum (and gas) shall be undertaken solely by the state ... and shall be implemented solely by state enterprises ... who may in turn reach work agreements with various contractors to implement this work where the state enterprise is unable to carry it out.' After the enactment of this Law three national oil companies were created (Permina, Pertamin and Permigan). This, and the subsequent Law No. 8 of 1971, still constitute the basic legal structure for the exploration and exploitation of oil and gas and the prime basis on which relationships with foreign and national companies have, at least, to be seen to be handled.[11]

The concession rights of the foreign oil companies were revoked when the new Mining Law was brought in. However, their continued operation as contractors for the state under new 'contract of work' (Perjanjian Karya) agreements was provided for. Indeed they were given priority in converting their operations to the new contractual arrangements.

Clearly the government had to accept that the expertise and capital of the existing foreign oil companies were still required and that the state oil companies were not yet ready to take on a major role. Sukarno's anti-western and anti-capitalist attitudes had to be balanced against the desperate need to expand oil exports as a bolster for an increasingly ailing economy. He faced considerable difficulty in resisting proposals for extreme legislation and in dampening down the militancy of the trade unions and communist party towards the oil companies.

Negotiations had been going on between the government and the three international companies over their future status as contractors since the passing of the 1960 Law. Indonesia joined OPEC on 4 June, 1962 and in a more aggressive and difficult climate the government began negotiating with the international oil companies for 60 per cent of oil industry profits. A somewhat bitter confrontation ensued. This was partly resolved, after exchanges of ultimata between the Indonesian government and the American companies and thanks to the intervention of the US Kennedy administration, by the signing of the 'Tokyo Agreement' in June 1963. This agreement introduced new terms to be incorporated into the contracts of work with the three companies involved. Each of the three foreign companies gave up their old concession rights and in exchange were awarded 20-year contracts and agreed to act as contractors to one of the three state oil companies active at the time. In exchange they were awarded 20-year contracts to continue development in the old concession areas. Perhaps more significantly they were permitted to make applications for 30-year contracts to explore and develop new areas adjacent to their existing concessions. Contracts for the new areas required immediate payments of cash bonuses with continued tenure subject to the expenditure of $15 million over eight years for each area. Additional payments were required when commercial production was established. There was also, amongst other conditions, the Indonesianization of staff.

An earlier contract had already been signed in mid-1962 with Pan American, a newcomer to Indonesia. It included a provision for a 60/40 split of net profits in favour of the state; the profit division to be made after current operating expenses had been met and exploration costs written off at 10 per cent per annum. Another key feature was that profit was to be calculated on the basis of prices realized in selling the crude oil rather than using posted prices. This was a most significant contract and a breakthrough for the government in its confrontation with the companies which put immediate pressure on the original three, and set the tone for the negotiation of subsequent agreements.

The new terms obliged the oil companies to relinquish their existing concessions to the government. Although the companies were apparently turned into contractors for the state companies there was, in practice, little difference from the traditional concession system in many aspects of the arrangements. Significantly, the foreign contractors retained management control and were allowed to operate in new areas. The innovation, which was later to become a widely accepted model in other countries, was that all financial arrangements were expressed in terms of oil as shares of production to be received by the foreign companies and by the state-owned companies. The contractors financed all operations and, if successful, received oil to cover their costs and depreciation charges and retained 40 per cent of net profits from the operation. This was free of taxes.

The foreign companies were authorized to take over the government's share of production and were being appointed as exclusive sales agents to market oil accruing to the state enterprises. The government, however, reserved the right to elect to take 20 per cent of aggregate gross production in kind. This latter provision had the effect of assuring the Indonesian government of at least some income from production under the contract. The foreign company paid the value of this share to the state company with title to the oil changing hands at the point of export.[12]

Export income was assessed for profit sharing on the basis of prevailing market prices for sales to third-party customers. Indonesia's acceptance of a market-related 'realized' revenue base, and agreed levels of cost recovery, was a further innovation which contrasted significantly with the system then employed by Middle Eastern OPEC members of using administered posted prices for revenue purposes. This relieved the companies of the kind of tension associated with their Venezuelan and Middle Eastern operations caused by royalty and tax obligations being related to posted prices at a time when discounting in the market place was common.

The sale of all Shell and Stanvac's refineries and of all three companies' marketing and distribution facilities was also stipulated in their new work contracts. These conditions were not perhaps as onerous to the companies as they seemed. Price controls had operated since 1945 and inflation had rendered the fixed price for product sales unrealistic. The companies had tended to carry their losses by the more profitable trade in the export of products to other South East Asian countries. The refineries were also a vulnerable high profile symbol of foreign oil in the difficult and dangerous political climate of the time. Subsequently, as a result of severe labour difficulties and other problems, Shell sold or transferred its entire operations to state companies Permina and Pertamin, and withdrew from Indonesia in 1965. Shell was paid largely in oil and its employees remained in Indonesia under a service contract. The takeover of Stanvac and Caltex marketing facilities, also by Pertamin, took place rapidly during 1964 and 1965.

The work contract was seen as primarily a profit-sharing arrangement with payment in financial terms. The basic government objective of asserting its ownership of petroleum resources was achieved but, in practice, this was somewhat symbolic. Full management rights and control over operations remained with the foreign company and there was little provision for effective supervision. The government, however, thanks to the flexibility of its approach, managed to obtain a larger revenue share than under previous arrangements and provide at the same time incentives for some much needed development. These new contracts prevented a precipitous withdrawal of the foreign companies. They provided the companies with terms that were no less favourable than those currently available in the Middle East. The introduction of the work contract also paved the way, and was the basis for, the development of the production-sharing contract which was eventually to dominate contractual arrangements in Indonesia.

Production, based largely on the Minas and Duri fields, increased steadily throughout the 1950s and early 1960s. By 1969, the Minas field had become one of the 22 fields in the world in which cumulative production had reached 1 billion barrels.

The general civil unrest and anti-foreign attitudes manifested themselves on the oilfields in wild cat strikes and takeovers by communist-led trade unions, causing the steady and substantial increase in production that had occurred through the 1950s to falter during the last years of Sukarno's presidency. Crude production fell in 1963 and 1966 although it recovered slightly in 1967 to reach just over 500,000 b/d. Exports of hydrocarbons still represented only 30 per cent of total exports and the country's share of oil production in the Far East had fallen to 50 per cent compared with 75 per cent before the Second World War. This fall in regional significance was partly due to the more rapid development of oil production elsewhere, particularly in China and India. No exploration had been done by the three main contractors in new areas for over 20 years! After independence, in August 1950 a motion had been passed by parliament to put a freeze on granting new concessions while a new oil policy was developed. This freeze lasted for ten years. Indeed, if Stanvac and Shell had been allowed to explore and develop new areas as they had wanted to during the 1950s and early 1960s overall national production may well not have stagnated. By not allowing exploration and development in new areas by the three existing international companies, nationalism dealt a severe blow to production and, ultimately, to the broader economy.

Sukarno's failures in managing the economy and internal politics and his increasingly egocentric and dictatorial behaviour were partly behind the communist takeover attempt in September 1965. The real significance and some of the details of the events involved in this attempted coup are still not known. What is clear is that executive power was transferred to General Suharto in March 1966 authorizing him to restore order, which he did at the cost of many lives. The ethnic Chinese suffered particularly badly; estimates of those murdered range from 100,000 to 1 million. This was in part an expression of long-held resentment at the apparent dominance of Chinese entrepreneurs and the paying off of old scores. The communist party was destroyed and remains suppressed; nationalist civilian politicians were removed from power and the army came into the ascendancy. Another result of these events was the reorganization of the oil industry and the strengthening of the state's oil instruments.

The enactment of the 1960 Oil Law in effect signalled the end of the old oil era in Indonesia. There were already three national oil companies in operation and available for increased state participation in the oil industry. With the eventual ascendancy of the army, Permina was developed as the dominant state oil enterprise responsible for production while the role of Pertamin was reduced. This formation of an all-embracing state oil company was a bold step much in advance of the other members of OPEC. Permina was formally merged with Pertamin in 1968 to form a single state hydrocarbon corporation, PT Pertamina. The third company, Permigan, had been dissolved in 1965.

Eventually, after a lengthy power struggle with Sukarno and his supporters, General Suharto became acting president and then president of the country in March 1968. When Sukarno died in 1970 a new order had begun.

## Stability and Growth: The Long Presidency

Since he was first elected in 1968, the now 74-year old Suharto has been re-elected for five further five-year terms of office. Thus, there have been only two presidents in the 45 years since independence.

Politically the country is a unitary state with an executive president elected by a People's Consultative Assembly.[13] The latter is designated under the constitution as the highest authority of the state; in practice the power lies elsewhere. The ruling

Golkar party is a government sponsored 'alliance of groups representing farmers, fishermen and the professions' with a strong military presence. It is backed by the civil service and has a distinct advantage over opposition groups in terms of funding and organization. Golkar provides a nominally civilian basis for what is in effect a military regime.[14]

Parliament itself is an ineffective counterbalance to the executive and an inadequate channel for popular feeling. The real balance of power lies outside Parliament and the political parties. The president, including his family and those who enjoy their patronage, the armed forces (known by the acronym **ABRI**), ethnic Chinese businessmen and Islam (the majority religion) all interact and compete to varying degrees. However, power really lies with the president and the armed forces. Recent cabinets have consisted of more civilians than military men and Suharto prefers to don a civilian image in public, but the basis of political power remains the army.

The political and military philosophy of the armed forces positively encourages involvement in politics. Military men, on both the active and retired lists, are spread throughout centres of commercial and political power and are allocated one-fifth of the seats in Parliament. There is a parallel military administration down to village level and the army plays the key role in holding the country together. It also guides and is very deeply involved in the development of the economy and many aspects of commerce including the energy business.

Stability and cohesion have been maintained successfully through the long years of Suharto's presidency to the present day. This has been partly through strong central control based on Java which has, at times, shown itself capable of extreme ruthlessness in crushing dissent. However, social progress and stability would not have been sustained over the years without considerable success in achieving substantial economic growth combined with the help of the official philosophy of 'live and let live'. This state philosophy, the Pancasila,[15] originally expounded by Sukarno as a means of uniting the diverse elements of the archipelago, emphasizes religious tolerance, unity in diversity and justice. Clearly some actions of the Indonesian government show that Pancasila has its limits and it is easy to be cynical about the reality behind such state sponsored slogans.

Nonetheless, in the context of Indonesia and the Indonesian temperament, this official line seems to be sincerely meant. The mental flexibility and moral tolerance that it implies appear, up to now, to have had an effect in reducing tension between the ethnic Chinese and the indigenous majority, between Java and the rest of the islands, and between the religious and other factions.

Under Suharto, Indonesia in the late 1960s turned away from isolationism and confrontation. It rejoined the United Nations and re-established relations with bodies such as the World Bank, the IMF and OECD. It became a founder member of the Association of South East Asian Nations (ASEAN)[16] and made a determined and successful effort to attract foreign investment.

In the mid-1960s Indonesia had been a centrally controlled and bankrupt economy with a strongly nationalistic foreign policy. Annual real growth in GDP is believed to have averaged only about 2 per cent during the period 1950 to 1966. This was lower than the growth in population so that real income per head in 1966 was probably lower than in 1950. The establishment of the 'New Order' government by Suharto put in place a series of measures in the late 1960s which helped to set the country fairly quickly on to a new and increasingly successful course of economic development. These measures included allowing the return of foreign investment through joint ventures and guarantees on repatriation of profits. Cuts were made in government expenditure, rice prices were held in check through the use of a reserve and there was some success in stabilizing the prices of other basic commodities. The country also benefited from the growing presence of western educated technocrats in the administration.

A new framework for national economic planning was also instituted in 1969, in the form of five-year development plans or Pelita. Although very detailed in their targets[17] they are, in practice, much less rigid and constraining than the models favoured in the old Eastern Bloc economies. Certainly, their targets seem usually not to be too far removed from what can be realistically achieved. The Pelita still go into a great deal of detail but they seem to play a less significant role now the country is becoming increasingly an open economy.

During the early 1970s, most of the development portion of

the budget still came from foreign aid. In 1969 at the start of the first Pelita, 80 per cent of development expenditure was financed by foreign aid. By 1976, this proportion had been reduced to 35 per cent. Economic progress came to rely heavily on Indonesia's success in developing its oil and gas resources and on the vagaries of the international oil market. The introduction of the contract of work and the subsequent development of the production-sharing contract (PSC) in the 1960s formed the basis for the expansion of the oil and gas production that was vital for the growth of the economy. The development and significance of the production-sharing agreements are covered in Chapter 2. The hydrocarbon industry in Indonesia is now much less important than in the boom years of the 1970s thanks to successful economic diversification policies. Indeed, at the OPEC meeting in Bali in November 1994, President Suharto told the assembled delegates that oil 'no longer plays an important role' in the Indonesian economy. Nonetheless, the country's continued development and the well-being of its people are still very closely linked with the fortunes of oil and gas and will remain so well into the next century.

Revenues from hydrocarbons were already growing in importance as the basis for development in the later part of the 1960s but were most prominent in the years from 1973 to 1981. By 1970, the value of oil exports had doubled from that of a decade earlier and oil's share of exports had already reached 40 per cent. On the eve of the international oil price increases of 1973–4, oil's share of exports was nearly 50 per cent. Then, Indonesia found itself the unexpected beneficiary of the boom in international oil prices.

By 1975, hydrocarbon exports were well over 70 per cent of total exports and were to reach a peak in 1981 of nearly 80 per cent. The rapid increase in the value of oil revenues after 1973–4 and 1979 was, of course, due largely to the OPEC induced price rises. There was, however, some increase in export volumes up to 1979 which also helped; the subsequent decline in volumes was offset for a few years by the 1979–80 price rises.

The period from the late 1960s to 1981 was a remarkable one in the economic growth of Indonesia. It was an era of economic rehabilitation and growth made possible by the oil derived foreign exchange bonanza, although foreign aid was still important. The average rate of growth in GDP accelerated to well over 7 per cent per annum and only dropped below 6 per cent in 1 year out of 14 between 1967 and 1981. By 1981, the economy had improved sufficiently for the country to be reclassified by the World Bank into the ranks of the lower middle income countries. These were the years of the 'oil boom'.

Economic growth had begun to accelerate well before the dramatic increases in world oil prices of 1973 and therefore cannot be entirely attributed to a rapid growth in oil earnings. Much of the growth which occurred in the oil boom period was also due to increases in the labour supply and in real investment supported by substantial international loans. Unlike many other OPEC countries, Indonesia spent relatively little of its foreign exchange bounty on imports of consumer goods. However, it did substantially increase its imports of raw materials and intermediate products. Growth in the manufacturing sector was mainly into the final stages of production of imported raw materials and components to be sold on the domestic market. It was therefore vulnerable to falls in oil revenues which would reduce the capacity to import. More generally, as economic growth stemmed to some extent from improvement in the terms of trade, the subsequent deterioration in the relative prices of oil exports to imports was found to have an adverse impact on the national income.

Through the 1970s and early 1980s, Indonesia came to depend very heavily on its foreign exchange earnings and domestic budgetary revenues from the oil and gas sector (see Table 1.3). The substantial flow of funds from oil exports gave a major boost to the financial and construction sectors as foreign investment flowed into the country and numerous development projects were launched. Although there were some extravagant and probably unnecessary projects, the government was relatively prudent in managing its new wealth.

Paradoxically, it was at the height of the oil boom that Pertamina, the state oil company, ran into serious difficulties. Pertamina had been a pacesetter for other industries during the late 1960s and early 1970s and one which had contributed enormously to the successes of the period. Unfortunately, it overreached itself. Its borrowing tactics, the range of its operations and the manner in which they were conducted were

**Table 1.3**: Annual Average Real Foreign Exchange Inflows. Per Cent

|  | *1968–1972* | *1973–1981* | *1982–1989* |
|---|---|---|---|
| Export Oil | 30 | 64 | 52 |
| Other | 43 | 24 | 31 |
| Net Government Aid and Borrowings | 17 | 11 | 13 |
| Direct Investment and Other Net Private Inflows | 10 | 1 | 4 |
| Total | 100 | 100 | 100 |
| (Million US $ 1975 Prices) | 3,081 | 12,438 | 13,194 |

Source: A. Booth, *The Oil Boom and After*, 1992

imprudent to say the least. It was officially announced that, as of March 1975, Pertamina owed $3.1 billion in foreign loans and overdue oil revenue payments to the government as well as $113 million in sums overdue to local contractors. Total debts for the 1976 fiscal year were stated by the then Minister of Mines to have reached over $10 billion.[18] Not unexpectedly, there were recriminations and the curtailing of Pertamina's operations followed (see Chapter 6). Pertamina's financial policies caused a setback to the Indonesian economy as funds that would have gone to development had to be used to repay the debts. Foreign reserves fell considerably.

One beneficial effect of the Pertamina affair was to strengthen the hands of those advocating a more balanced and managed economic development and to dampen down the rush into capital-intensive, high-technology projects. The adverse effects of this incident on the economy were overcome remarkably quickly and eventually resulted in a much improved climate for development. The company's external debts in March 1992 were down to $0.4 billion.

It can be seen from Table 1.4 that the importance of hydrocarbons to the economy reached its peak in 1981. In that year, 80 per cent of the country's export earnings and around 70 per cent of domestically generated fiscal revenues were obtained from oil and gas. Currently only around 30 per cent of export earnings and 30 per cent of revenues come from hydrocarbons.

**Table 1.4:** Contribution of Oil and Gas to Total Exports

| Year | Exports of Oil and Gas US $ Billion | Percentage of Total Exports |
|---|---|---|
| 1960 | 0.2 | 26 |
| 1970 | 0.4 | 40 |
| 1971 | 0.6 | 47 |
| 1972 | 1.0 | 54 |
| 1973 | 1.7 | 50 |
| 1974 | 5.1 | 70 |
| 1975 | 5.0 | 73 |
| 1976 | 6.1 | 71 |
| 1977 | 7.3 | 68 |
| 1978 | 7.4 | 68 |
| 1979 | 9.7 | 51 |
| 1980 | 15.7 | 72 |
| 1981 | 17.7 | 80 |
| 1982 | 15.0 | 79 |
| 1983 | 13.8 | 73 |
| 1984 | 15.2 | 72 |
| 1985 | 12.8 | 68 |
| 1986 | 8.0 | 55 |
| 1987 | 8.8 | 51 |
| 1988 | 8.3 | 42 |
| 1989 | 8.5 | 38 |
| 1990 | 11.8 | 45 |
| 1991 | 11.6 | 40 |
| 1992 | 10.4 | 31 |
| 1993 | 9.5 (est) | 30 |

Sources: *IFS Yearbook*, 1992; *Indonesia: Source Book*, 1993

The progressive weakening of international oil markets from the end of 1981 onwards imposed increasingly severe constraints on the economy (see Table 1.5). Both export earnings and fiscal revenues were reduced as prices fell and oil exports declined and stagnated – the latter being effected largely by rising domestic consumption and falling production. In 1982, GDP grew by only 2.2 per cent after having grown by 7.9 per cent in the previous year and by some measures actually declined. Growth was fairly erratic through much of the remainder of the 1980s. The substantial reduction in growth in 1982 was directly due to a sharp fall in oil production from 1.6 million

**Table 1.5:** Falling Oil Prices and Oil Production

| Year | Crude Oil Production (1) | Oil Exports (2) | Official Selling Price (3) | GDP Growth (Constant Prices) |
|------|------|------|------|------|
| | | (Million b/d) | ($ Per bbl. f.o.b.) | Per Cent Per Annum |
| 1970 | 0.9 | 0.7 | 1.70 | |
| 1975 | 1.3 | 1.2 | 12.80 | 7.7 |
| 1978 | 1.65 | 1.4 | 13.55 | (1971–1980) |
| 1980 | 1.6 | 1.2 | 29.50 | |
| 1981 | 1.7 | 1.2 | 35.00 | 7.9 |
| 1982 | 1.4 | 0.9 | 34.53 | 2.2 |
| 1983 | 1.4 | 1.0 | 29.53 | 4.2 |
| 1984 | 1.5 | 1.1 | 29.53 | 7.0 |
| 1985 | 1.3 | 0.9 | 29.53 | 2.5 |
| 1986 | 1.4 | 1.0 | 29.53 | 5.9 |
| 1987 | 1.4 | 0.9 | 17.15 | 10.5 |
| 1988 | 1.3 | 0.9 | 17.15 | 5.8 |
| 1989 | 1.4 | 0.9 | 17.49 | 7.5 |
| 1990 | 1.5 | 0.9 | 17.49 | 7.2 |
| 1991 | 1.7 | 1.1 | 17.72 | 6.9 |
| 1992 | 1.6 | 1.1 | 17.35 | 6.4 |
| 1993 | 1.6 | 1.0 | 16.07 | 6.5 |
| 1994 (Est.) | 1.5 | 1.0 | 16.58 | 6.7 |

(1)   Including NGLs
(2)   Crude Oil and Products
(3)   Minas Crude

Sources: *Asian Development Outlook; Twentieth Century Petroleum Statistics; OPEC Statistical Bulletin; Oil and Energy Trends;* IMF, *IFS Yearbook,* 1992; *Indonesia: Source Book,* 1993; *Petroleum Report of Indonesia,* 1993

barrels per day (mb/d) to 1.3 mb/d. This was a result of complying with OPEC mandated production levels although capacity may have fallen. Poor performances in agriculture and manufacturing and less favourable terms of trade also contributed.

Diminished oil production reduced government revenues and strained the policy of using production-sharing crude for subsidized sales of petroleum products to the domestic market. As a result subsidies were cut in 1982–3 and domestic fuel prices increased by 60 to 75 per cent.

The real impact of falling oil prices was mitigated for a time by the appreciation of the US dollar used for pricing oil and gas exports. The beneficial effect of an appreciating dollar was due to the fact that whilst some 90 per cent of export earnings was then denominated in dollars, most external commitments were in non-dollar currencies. At the same time, there was a major expansion of LNG exports, which grew between 1980 and 1984 by 78 per cent or 14 bcm. This and the stabilization of oil production helped to offset falling prices. The early 1980s was also the time when rice production increased very significantly and self-sufficiency was achieved. The result, for example, was that GDP in 1984 grew in real terms at 7 per cent. Clearly oil was no longer the sole major indigenous arbiter of the country's economic fortunes.

Oil exports had already started to decline in 1978, but the effect had been ameliorated for some years by the high oil prices. The fall in international oil prices that occurred during 1986 came as crude oil production had already fallen back to nearly 400,000 b/d below the peak levels of the second half of the 1970s. The terms offered to international oil companies under the production-sharing contracts had not apparently been such as to attract adequate investment in developing new fields and providing new technology. Subsequently, changes were made to the terms of the contracts, in 1988, 1989 and 1992, and some new forms of contract were introduced (see Chapter 2). The situation was exacerbated by the sharp decline in the value of the dollar that had occurred after 1985. In 1986, the value of oil and gas exports fell to US $8 billion compared with nearly US $18 billion in 1981 and stayed between US $8 to 9 billion during the rest of the 1980s.

At the same time as the international oil market weakened dramatically, the markets for Indonesia's other export commodities were also facing considerable volatility. The value of gas exports fell because of indexation to falling oil prices and the renegotiation of pricing formulae in this depressed context. The government was forced to make substantial changes to its economic policy in general and to its industrialization policy in particular.

The high oil prices of the 1970s had led to a boom in development projects, some of them unsuitable and uncompetitive. A major new programme for long overdue expansion and upgrading of the oil refineries was initiated. Subsequently, in the face of a weak oil market, severe revenue volatility in most other export commodities and a changed international business climate, substantial adjustments to economic policy had to be made. To this end, a general restructuring of the economy away from heavy reliance on oil and gas exports was begun in the second half of the 1980s.

The end of the oil boom, although presenting difficulties, acted as a very useful stimulus to the introduction of reforms that had long been felt necessary. The process of economic restructuring began in 1982–3 with several new initiatives in monetary, fiscal and exchange rate policies. Several large public sector industrial projects, including the refineries and petrochemical plants, were rescheduled in order to ease the burden on the budget and the rupiah was devalued in March 1983.

As a way of promoting its non-oil domestic revenues and a more export-oriented trade regime, the government introduced a number of major economic reforms. The tax system was completely overhauled and tariffs rationalized and a series of measures, taken mainly in the 1980s, resulted in extensive liberalization of the financial sector. In addition, over this period subsidies were gradually lifted from most parts of the economy and customs, port handling and shipping procedures were reformed. Such measures helped to convince the outside world that the government was serious in wanting to change its policies towards business. The policy of import restrictions rather than active export promotion for non-oil commodities and manufacturers was continued until the sharp decline in international oil prices in early 1986. This event stimulated the government to introduce a wide-ranging package of measures to facilitate the purchase of imports at world prices by firms producing in whole or in part for export. There was another substantial devaluation of the rupiah in September 1986, primarily intended to improve the competitiveness of Indonesian exports and encourage domestic producers to begin selling on the world market. The government was very successful in controlling inflation after both the devaluations, which helped to bring about a large and sustained fall in the real exchange rate.

A start was also made at around this time on establishing performance criteria for state enterprises with the aim of deciding what form their ownership and control should take in future. Despite many obstacles and rigidities, economic performance through the 1980s was creditable and progress was much more substantial than in the difficult years of the 1960s. Between 1981 and 1990, growth in GDP averaged 5.5 per cent. The advances in agriculture, the building up of the physical infrastructure and the managerial and technical capabilities that had occurred in the years of the oil boom, undoubtedly helped to prevent the 1980s from being an economic disaster.

Over the last 20 years, 1973 to 1993, economic growth has averaged just over 6 per cent per annum. Such high rates of growth allied with political stability have enabled great strides to be made in reducing poverty, improving health and building up a modern infrastructure. Only 17 per cent of the population are currently said to be below the official poverty line and adult illiteracy was down to 23 per cent in 1990 compared with 61 per cent in 1960.[19] This is the fourth lowest rate of all the lower income countries and a remarkable achievement given the size and diversity of the country. A series of deregulations and reforms has now opened up strategic industries to foreign investment, allowing broader ownership rights in export-oriented manufacturing industries.

Non-oil exports are now increasing at a rapid rate; by 26 per cent in 1992 and 24 per cent the year before. This is a very creditable performance given the slowing down of the world's major economies. GDP is believed to have grown at just under 6.5 per cent in 1993 and at around 6.7 per cent in 1994 although inflation seems to have nearly doubled to almost 10 per cent. The government looks well on target to achieving its goal of 'middle income' country status.

The contribution of the oil and gas sector to total domestic revenues is now under 30 per cent, compared with 66 per cent in the year 1984/85 (see Table 1.6). Nonetheless, the hydrocarbon industry is still the largest single contributor to government revenue. The fastest growing revenue source is income tax and it is expected that in the current financial year, tax revenues will exceed those from oil for the first time.

The fall in the use of government revenues by the oil sector in the form of fuel subsidies reflects the positive government action on fuel prices that was taken during the early 1980s,

**Table 1.6**: The Contribution of the Oil and Gas Sector to Government Revenues

| Year | Revenues from Oil and Gas as Per Cent of Domestic Revenues | Fuel Subsidy as Per Cent of Total Domestic Revenues |
|---|---|---|
| 1979/1980 | 64 | 8 |
| 1984/1985 | 66 | 3 |
| 1989/1990 | 39 | 2 |
| 1990/1991 | 27 | 2 |
| 1991/1992 | 29 | 3 |
| 1992/1993 | 30 | 2 |
| 1993/1994 (Est.) | 29 | 2 |

Source: *Petroleum Report of Indonesia*, 1993

even before the oil price shocks of 1986. Subsidies on domestic oil products became lower in unit terms and less widespread than in the 1970s. In the 1993/94 budget, the government at last felt confident enough to move a long way towards abolishing all fuel subsidies. As a result, fuel prices were raised between 5 and 27 per cent, while electricity and transport tariffs are expected to increase by an average of 13 per cent and 10 per cent respectively. By the end of the current Pelita early in 1999, it is expected that all domestic oil prices will reflect true border prices.

Net foreign exchange earnings from oil and gas are now running at around $9 billion per annum, a significant improvement on much of the late 1980s. The growing importance of LNG as a source of foreign exchange is clear from Table 1.7. Indeed, in net terms, the contribution from gas is now roughly the same as from oil.

Unfortunately, the cost of oil imports has also risen in recent years to offset export earnings (see Table 1.8). Imports in 1992 included around 105,000 b/d of oil products, largely middle distillates, to make up the product imbalance, and 108,000 b/d of Middle East crude for the Cilacap refinery. Following the earlier expansion, a substantial increase in both domestic and export orientated refineries was planned for the 1990s to eliminate the need for oil product imports and to upgrade exports. The placing of a ceiling on foreign debt in late 1991 in an attempt to cool an overheated economy had the effect of

**Table 1.7**: Draft State Budget 1993/1994. Revenues in Trillions of Rupiahs

| Domestic Revenues | 1993/1994 | Increase/Decrease over Previous Year |
|---|---|---|
| Oil | 11.8 | + 5.4 |
| LNG | 3.3 | +20.9 |
| Income Tax | 14.8 | +35.9 |
| VAT | 11.7 | + 5.9 |
| Import Duties | 3.1 | + 2.1 |
| Excise Tax | 2.5 | + 2.3 |
| Sales of Oil Products | 0.2 | -73.8 |
| Land and Building Taxes | 1.3 | +33.3 |
| Other Taxes etc. | 4.1 | |
| | | |
| *Development Revenues* | | |
| Programme Aid | 0.4 | -14.8 |
| Project Aid | 9.1 | 0.3 |
| | | |
| *Total Revenues* | 62.3 | 11.1 |

Source: *Indonesian Development Quarterly*, various issues

**Table 1.8**: Foreign Exchange Earnings from Oil and Gas. $ Billion

| Oil | 1988/89 | 1990/91 | 1991/92 | 1992/93 | 1993/94 |
|---|---|---|---|---|---|
| Exports f.o.b. | 5.0 | 8.1 | 6.9 | 6.4 | 5.5 |
| Imports f.o.b. | -1.9 | -3.4 | -2.8 | -3.3 | -3.1 |
| Services | -1.6 | -1.8 | -1.6 | -1.7 | -1.7 |
| Sub Total | 1.5 | 2.9 | 2.5 | 1.4 | 1.7 |
| | | | | | |
| *Gas* | | | | | |
| Exports f.o.b. | 2.7 | 4.7 | 3.8 | 3.6 | 3.9 |
| Imports f.o.b. | -0.2 | -0.2 | -0.2 | -0.3 | -0.3 |
| Services | -1.0 | -1.4 | -1.3 | -1.3 | -1.4 |
| Sub Total | 1.5 | 3.1 | 2.3 | 2.0 | 2.2 |
| Net Oil/Gas Trade | 3.0 | 6.0 | 4.8 | 3.4 | 2.9 |
| Net Non-Oil/Gas Trade | -4.9 | -9.8 | -9.1 | -5.7 | -5.7 |

Source: *Petroleum Report of Indonesia*, 1994

postponing and cancelling a number of the refinery projects. For this reason, it will be some years before the need for net product imports is eliminated.

Natural gas is usually forecast to take over much of oil's role as a source of export revenue into the next century. However, progress in this direction has in recent years been painfully slow. Much of the relative increase in the importance of gas exports actually occurred in the early 1980s as the major contracts built up and prices were firm. In fact, in the mid-1980s, gas exports made up about 35 per cent of total oil and gas exports and this is still roughly the current proportion. Through much of the late 1980s the number of cargoes continued to increase but the total value of exports fell or stagnated. Indeed, the value of gas exports relative to oil exports declined through much of this period and only picked up again in the early 1990s.

The opening of the planned new LNG trains over the next few years seems likely to provide partial compensation for the possibility of falling oil exports. A more substantial contribution to the economy rests upon the adequacy and feasibility of the gas reserves and their ability to support an expansion into new markets as well as a renewal of existing LNG contracts. It does, of course, also depend on the potential existence of substantial new export outlets for Indonesian gas in South East Asia and the willingness of the international community to make available the very substantial capital that will be required (see Chapter 4).

The development of indigenous coal production for export through foreign investment was encouraged during the 1980s as one approach to diversification. After some false starts and delays, Indonesia has now become the world's fourth largest coal exporter, although the contribution to export earnings is still very modest in comparison with oil and gas.

Oil and gas will continue to play a major role in the economy of Indonesia for many years although its contribution to national income is now exceeded by both agriculture and manufacturing. However, even if oil production levels were to increase modestly, which is by no means certain, the role of oil as a source of export revenues must inevitably continue to decline as domestic demand for oil increases. Indeed, Indonesia could under some scenarios become a net oil importer within the next ten years or so (see Chapter 3).

As a result of determined effort and increasingly realistic economic policies, the economy no longer has the overwhelming dependency on oil and gas exports that once made it so vulnerable. This is just as well. The contribution of oil and gas exports together is unlikely to increase significantly unless there is a sharp and sustained rise in prices, which for the next few years at least seems unlikely. Nonetheless, the encouragement of new oil and gas development, the maintenance of oil exports and the expansion of markets for gas, remain absolutely essential to support the pace of development necessary for the country's well-being.

## Notes

1.  Anthropologists have identified over 300 language groups, many with fully developed scripts and long traditions of written literature. Although widely spoken, local languages are now almost universally supplanted by Indonesia's national language, Bahasa Indonesia. This is formed from the regional Malay language but greatly enriched with other vocabularies. Religious beliefs range from the intensely Islamic people of Aceh on the northern tip of Sumatra to the Christians of East Timor and the primitive animist tribes of Irian Jaya in the far east of the archipelago. *The Economist*, 17 April, 1993.

2.  Indonesia has, in the past, usually been recorded as consisting of 13,667 islands or parts of islands. However, new methods of satellite mapping have boosted the number to 17,508. National Development Information Office (NDIO), *Indonesia: Source Book*, 1993.

3.  The last independent oil company, Dordsche Petroleum Maatschapping was absorbed in 1911. *Petroleum Report of Indonesia*, 1982.

4.  Standard of New Jersey was the first US company to receive a concession. In 1933 it reached an agreement with Socony Vacuum (later Mobil) which controlled the former Standard Oil marketing network in the Far East to form Stanvac as an equally owned subsidiary. Stanvac took over its parent companies' upstream and downstream interests in Asia. Standard Oil of California (Chevron) became the second US company to obtain concessions and in 1936 sold a 50 per cent share to Texaco as part of the agreement to form their jointly owned California Texas Oil Company (Caltex).

5.  BPM had six refineries, two in each of the main producing areas of Sumatra, Java and Kalimantan whilst NKPM had a refinery in Sumatra and another on Java. The crude from the NIAM fields was treated in the BPM refineries. *Twentieth Century Petroleum Statistics*, various issues.

6.  The initial configuration was a confederation of semi autonomous states. On 1 May, 1963 the additional territory of Irian Jaya (West New Guinea) was transferred to Indonesia from the Netherlands. The Portuguese colony of East Timor was taken over forcibly by Indonesia in the face of world opinion to become its twenty-seventh province in July 1976.

7.  Partai Komunisi Indonesia (PKI). This was a distinctly Indonesian style movement which grew to be well organized and disciplined and in 1965

claimed to have some 20 million members. It apparently came very close to seizing power before its almost complete destruction by the army in 1965. R. Mortimer, *Indonesian Communism under Sukarno*, 1974.

8.   The agreements referred exclusively to the disposition of foreign exchange earnings from the export of products and crude oil. It was recognized that if the companies withdrew, fresh investments would not be easily forthcoming. The 'let alone' agreements in effect allowed the companies to retain their foreign exchange earnings for an agreed number of years on condition that they made no demands on the government's foreign exchange fund for rebuilding the industry or extending oil production. Thus, the companies were rebuilding the industry from their own overseas financial resources. Stanvac was successful in signing a new four-year 'let alone' agreement in March 1954 which included tax arrangements approximating to the 50/50 formula that other producing countries had established. Later agreements with Caltex and Shell also followed the pattern of the Stanvac agreement. S. Carlson, *Indonesia's Oil*, 1977; B. Glassburner et al, *The Economy of Indonesia*, 1971.

9.   Soon after independence, Indonesia decided to postpone the granting of concessions and development permits. Its attitude had hardened by 1957 when Parliament passed a resolution stopping new leases from being granted. The international companies were therefore solely dependent on their existing pre-war concessions.

10.  Technical and financial assistance contracts between Permina and the Japanese Group, the North Sumatran Oil Development Cooperation Company were signed in 1960. B. Glassburner et al, *The Economy of Indonesia*.

11.  The full Law No. 44 has almost nothing to say on any more detailed aspects of arrangements between the government and foreign companies. It is mainly about relations between the government and the state enterprises through which the government operates.

12.  Up to 25 per cent of each contractor's output also had to be supplied to the domestic market at cost price plus a small per barrel fee.

13.  The Consultative Assembly consists of all 500 members of the House of People's Representatives (of whom 100 are nominees of the armed forces) and an additional 500 appointed members such as representatives of the regions and functional groups. *Indonesia: Source Book*, 1993.

14.  There are two other officially recognized political parties; the Muslim United Development Party (PPP) and the Indonesian Democratic Party (PDI) but distinctions between these and the Golkar have been deliberately blurred. The communist party is outlawed.

15.  The five principles of Pancasila are; belief in one supreme God; justice and civility amongst people; the unity of Indonesia; democracy through deliberation and consensus amongst representatives: social justice for all. *Indonesia: Source Book*, 1993. The principle of social justice in basic terms is the provision of food and clothing for all. Democracy is intended to be the ideal of village democracy under a headman.

16.  The other members are Singapore, Thailand, Malaysia, the Philippines

and Brunei. Trade between members has not taken off as hoped and there is still not a great deal of cooperation on energy matters, although there are a number of proposals for joint energy projects such as an ASEAN gas network. A free trade area (AFTA) with systematic tariff reductions was launched on 1 January, 1993 and could eventually offer substantial economic benefits. In December 1994, Indonesia hosted the Asia Pacific Economic Co-operation (APEC) summit which aimed to expand free trade across the Pacific. *Indonesia Quarterly*, Winter 1993; *Financial Times*, 3 November, 1994.

17. For oil, for example, they include goals for refinery output, the volume of individual product exports and the number of wells to be drilled. The saving grace is that the targets are usually fairly realistic and not seen as absolutes. The current plan is the sixth (from 1994/95 to 1998/99). It assumes an average growth in oil consumption over this period of 5 per cent per annum. *The Economist*, various issues.

18. Sutowo emphasized the importance of spending heavily to build a modern technologically advanced industry whose skills would filter into other economic sections; on the other hand, some US-educated technocrats have placed great emphasis on spending available resources on programmes to create rural infrastructure, improve rice and other crop yields and encourage small labour-intensive industry. Derek Davies in the *Far Eastern Economic Review*, 30 May, 1975 quoted in 'Indonesia's Oil.' This conflict has persisted through the years with Dr Habibie, the current Minister for Research and Technology and chairman of the organization for the assessment and application of technology, now perhaps most closely representing the old Sutowo view.

19. Infant mortality has dropped from 128 per thousand in 1965 to 61 per thousand in 1990 and life expectancy has increased to 62 years. *World Development Report*, 1992.

## 2 THE DEVELOPMENT OF OIL PRODUCTION: THE FUTURE OF UPSTREAM OIL

### Introduction

The fear that, as domestic consumption of oil grows and production weakens, Indonesia will become a net importer of oil has been a consistent theme running through energy policy for some years. In the mid-1970s, it was said that at the rate of development projected by Pertamina and according to the then current reserve estimates, Indonesian oil for export would run out by 1992.[1] As with many similar views expressed about oil potential in other countries, this did not come to pass. However, the fears are still expressed, for example in 1993: 'Indonesia is likely to become a net importer of oil within the next ten years or so as domestic consumption grows and production falls.'[2] Or, at the end of 1994, 'Indonesia is about to lose its status as a net oil exporter.'[3]

It is rarely possible to be definite about future oil demand and supply for any country and this is particularly the case for such a large, diverse and relatively undeveloped country as Indonesia. It is nevertheless important to have a clear view of the current pattern of energy demand and supply and the way in which it may develop, in order to assess the likelihood and extent of an 'oil squeeze'. This would then indicate the constraints and opportunities involved in the energy economy of Indonesia and the direction in which energy policy has to travel. In this chapter we examine oil supply issues. The possible growth patterns of domestic demand for oil and the implications for the country's oil balance and for overall policy of these supply and demand factors are discussed in subsequent chapters.

### Oil Reserves and the Resource Base

The size of Indonesia's oil reserves and the overall extent of its oil resources are clearly of prime significance in determining possible future levels of oil production. The most important oil bearing and producing basins belong to the tertiary period. The oil prospects of the pre-tertiary are generally rated as poor although it is believed they could be rewarding in eastern

Indonesia where there have already been significant discoveries. Geological conditions in Indonesia are complex, with stable continental blocks, volcanic and non-volcanic island arcs and sedimentary basins of varying dimensions. It is also an area of strong crustal disturbances with recurring earth tremors and volcanic eruptions.

There are said to be 60 sedimentary basins spread across the Indonesian archipelago covering more than 2 million sq.km. of land and sea. Only some 38 of these have been subject to any kind of exploratory work and around 13 are currently under production. Many of the unexplored basins are in deep water and remote and rugged terrain and are expensive to explore and develop. Indonesia is not one of the world's easiest petroleum regions!

Estimates of proven reserves of oil, from a variety of sources and using different definitions, vary considerably as might be expected. They range between 5 and 21 billion barrels.[4] One accepted view, from the *Oil and Gas Journal*, is 5.8 billion barrels at the beginning of 1993 although this may not include condensates. Migas, the Indonesian Directorate of Oil and Gas, estimates remaining proven and potential reserves of oil to be just over 11 billion barrels of crude and condensate. Over 65 per cent of these reserves appear to be located in Central Sumatra (see Table 2.1).

**Table 2.1**:   Distribution of Proven and Potential Crude Oil and
Condensate Reserves.   Per Cent

| | |
|---|---|
| North Sumatra | 3.7 |
| Central Sumatra | 65.7 |
| South Sumatra | 4.8 |
| Natuna | 3.4 |
| West Java | 11.7 |
| East Java | 0.9 |
| East Kalimantan | 9.2 |
| Sulawesi | 0.1 |
| Irian Jaya | 0.5 |
| Total | 100.0 (11,295 Million Barrels) |

Source: *Petroleum Report of Indonesia*, 1993

This reserve estimate of 11 billion barrels contrasts with a cumulative production to date of just over 15 billion barrels spread over more than 100 years. Reserve estimates from the same sources have remained fairly consistent in the past. The authoritative journal *World Oil* put reserves at 8.2 billion in 1960, 10 billion in 1970, 10.5 billion in 1980 and 11.2 billion in 1990. Such stability of the reserve estimates through three decades during which oil production rose from 150 million barrels to 600 million barrels per year is indicative of the fluid and partly political nature of reserves estimates in general.[5]

The ratio of proven reserves to current production, that is how many years of production remain at current levels, stood at around 20 years for much of the 1980s. It appeared to rise in 1988 and 1989 to nearly 25 but is now down to just 11 years.

There is also, not unexpectedly, considerable uncertainty about the size of the overall resource base for oil. As mentioned, many potential oil-bearing basins have yet to be adequately explored and exploration has so far tended to be concentrated mainly in known producing areas. Partly as a result, there has been a wide range of estimates of the additional oil that might yet be discovered, from under 10 billion barrels to over 200 billion barrels.[6] Some of the higher estimates have probably been based on poor data and it is not always clear, for example, whether natural gas or gas liquids are included. Thus, any estimates of the size of the recoverable resource, including those in Table 2.2, need to be treated with great caution. Much more exploration needs to be undertaken in areas away from the existing major fields before a clearer picture of the volumes of oil

**Table 2.2**:   Indicative Resource Base. Billion Barrels of Oil (Including NGLs)

| | |
|---|---|
| Cumulative Production to End 1992 | 16 |
| Proven Reserves at 1 January, 1994 | 6 |
| Potential Reserves at 1 January, 1994 | 5 |
| Undiscovered | 50 |
| Total Recoverable Resource | 77 |

Sources: *Petroleum Report of Indonesia*, 1993, *World Oil*; *Twentieth Century Petroleum Statistics*

remaining to be exploited can be seen. An indicative estimate of the overall recoverable resource position is shown in Table 2.2.

There is a view that a considerable amount of additional oil remains to be proved up, the bulk of which is offshore. Many analysts believe that whilst west Indonesia is a mature oil province, the vast areas of eastern Indonesia hold the promise of significant discoveries of oil and gas. Despite the maturity of many of the fields that are currently producing, there is also scope for increased output through the application of secondary and tertiary recovery techniques. The question of how much economically recoverable oil might still be awaiting discovery or could be recovered by the application of new technology, however uncertain, is at the heart of the country's policies for hydrocarbons.

Total proven reserves of natural gas are said to be rather higher than those for oil; one estimate is around 2,500 to 2,800 bcm, the bulk of which is non-associated with oil. This is equivalent to 16–18 billion barrels of oil. The overall gas resource is sometimes put at between two to four times the reserve estimate. These types of numbers mean very little although it does seem likely that there are substantial volumes of gas yet to be discovered or proven up. The wide distribution of gas resources, the overall uncertainty about their potential and other aspects of gas development are discussed in Chapter 4.

As explained in subsequent chapters, it is imperative that sufficient reserves are proven up to keep Indonesia exporting substantial volumes of oil and gas well into the next century and at the same time meeting substantial growth in domestic demand. This will require much greater activity in offshore and remote areas than in the past.

The need to maintain and, if possible, to increase production, is reflected clearly in the government's approach to encouraging exploration and development throughout the history of Indonesia's hydrocarbon industry. This has often been refreshingly innovative and pragmatic – for example, in the successive additional incentives introduced into the production-sharing agreements and the new contractual bonuses for marginal areas. However, the changes needed sometimes seem to have been only grudgingly introduced; far too slowly and rather late in the day.

## The Development of Production Sharing and its Impact on Oil Production

The innovative agreement made in 1962 between Pan Am and Pertamin and the introduction in 1963 of new terms for the old concessionaires, Caltex, Stanvac and Shell as a result of the Tokyo Agreement, have been described in the previous chapter.

*Contracts of Work.* The key feature of the contracts of work was the division of the operating profits of the companies in the basic ratio of 60/40 in favour of the government. The 60 per cent profit share going to the government was agreed to include all forms of taxes applicable to the oil companies' operations. The 40 per cent going to the companies was thus 'clean' profit. As with the Pan Am contract, realized prices were used in the calculation of profit rather than posted prices.

The pre-Independence tax system that was continued under the 'let alone' agreements had consisted of a 4 per cent royalty on the well-head value of the crude oil produced, a 20 per cent profit tax (for the post-1928 concessions) and the application of a general corporate profits tax of 20 per cent. As a result, a company such as Stanvac with mainly post-1928 concessions would be paying at least 40 per cent of profits in tax under the old arrangements. Various additional taxes were also placed on exporting and marketing oil. This resulted in the companies claiming that, in the early 1950s, they were paying more than the conventional 50 per cent profit share applied by most oil-producing countries at the time. On this comparison with what had gone before, the contracts of work which allowed 40 per cent of profits retained free of tax and cost recovery, could be seen as not especially harsh.

However in late 1964 and early 1965, by appealing to nationalistic feeling pressure was brought to bear by various political elements against the companies from the old colonial era. The result was that in 1965, all foreign companies were placed under the control and supervision of the government. This involved representatives of the state oil companies, the Oil and Gas Directorate, senior Indonesian employees of the oil companies and trade union representatives. The communist party (PKI) was not, however, satisfied and called for the expropriation of the foreign companies. Although supervision as practised apparently did not induce much overt hostility to the foreign companies it was hardly conducive to attracting new investment. Downstream facilities were transferred much earlier than had been agreed under the contracts of work. Shell formally handed over all its upstream and downstream facilities on the last day of 1965 and withdrew completely from Indonesia. It was many years before it was to return to the country's oilfields. The events of 1965 represented a significant retreat from the position formally agreed in Tokyo.

The contracts of work had achieved the objective of asserting Indonesian ownership of hydrocarbons, whilst at the same time preventing a hasty withdrawal of all foreign activity. Despite everything it also encouraged some further development. The contracts did lead to a resumption of foreign investment by the two main contractors, Stanvac and Caltex. Much of the investment went to the existing Minas and Duri fields that were still at an early stage in their producing lives, that is on the rising part of their production curve. As a result there was a significant effect on overall production in the late-1960s (see Figure 2.1).

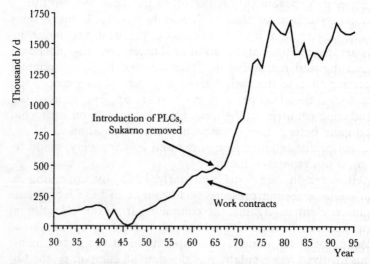

Sources:  *BP Statistical Review of World Energy; Oil and Energy Trends; Twentieth Century Petroleum Statistics*

**Figure 2.1**  Indonesian Oil Production 1930 to 1994

Although the contracts of work which replaced the inadequate 'let alone' agreements achieved the government's immediate objectives, they were in the nature of stop-gap measures. They certainly did little to address the need for greater exploration in new onshore areas and offshore. Stanvac was more seriously affected than Caltex because most of its available concessions were located in the already well exploited South Sumatran basin. Caltex, by contrast was more fortunate. Most of its concession acreage was in the Central Sumatran basin and its important discoveries of the Duri and Minas fields had been made just before the war. When Caltex regained possession of the fields in 1950, they still had the best years of development ahead of them. Minas and Duri remain today the largest producing fields in Indonesia and together currently contribute around 27 per cent of oil production. Caltex and Stanvac continued to operate in their original areas under contracts of work until they were converted to production-sharing contracts in 1993.

*Production-Sharing Contracts (PSC).* With production in the mid-1960s looking set to continue to stagnate, considerable effort needed to be put into opening up new potential oil-bearing areas and modernizing existing fields. Caltex and Stanvac still controlled most of the onshore production and investment by other companies was not forthcoming in any substantial measure. The uncertain political situation in Indonesia and the perceived hostile attitude of the government towards foreign oil companies were inhibiting factors. In addition, there was the restrictive legal framework for exploration and development provided by the contracts of work. The introduction of the production-sharing contracts was intended to fill this gap.

As early as 1960, Indonesia had established the initial basis for its claim to the offshore waters of the archipelago. This extended sovereignty over oil resources gave the state access to potential offshore production without jeopardizing the revenue rich onshore investments of the majors. The creation of the production-sharing contract also gave small independent oil companies access to these offshore resources without having to compete directly with the majors.

The principle of sharing the fruits of production between the landowner and the crop grower is as old as history and is still common in many agricultural societies. Production-sharing agreements were entered into by the Indonesians in the early 1960s with, for instance, a Japanese company for nickel extraction, and with an American company for fishing vessels and canning equipment. They were also used in certain circumstances by other countries, notably in South America. The introduction of production sharing to oil does, however, seem to have originated in Indonesia. Its development and application to the hydrocarbon industry by Ibnu Sutowu[7] is a prime example of the country's willingness to be flexible and innovative in balancing national aspirations with economic needs.[8]

The concept of production sharing was first mooted at a time of strong nationalism and xenophobia when there was a need for the government to uphold national ownership, exert real management and to direct. It came at a time when similar needs began to emerge in the Middle East and South America. Indonesia was somewhat ahead of the game, with a better split of profits (60/40 instead of the conventional 50/50) than other exporting countries, and a more flexible approach to the assessment of their profits (the use of market instead of posted prices). Independent oil companies saw in production sharing a tool that would break the majors' dominant access to good quality Indonesian crude. This was a period when US and Canadian independents were particularly interested in entering production areas overseas to gain increased supplies for their own refineries. For Japan, production sharing with their exploration companies such as Japex provided the opportunity to regain a foothold in the development of Indonesian oil. A number of circumstances and interests thus converged to create a fertile field for the introduction of production sharing to hydrocarbon development.

Nonetheless, even after the introduction of the PSC, Caltex was allowed in 1968 to extend its acreage in Central Sumatra under the old terms. This was a typical case of Indonesian pragmatism. Dr Sutowo was by then the President-Director of Pertamina and Director-General of the Bureau of Oil and Gas (Migas) and the leading protagonist for PSCs. However, he considered that Indonesia would receive more profits by letting an established company with lower development costs operate under the contract of work than allowing in a new company under a PSC.[9]

Initially the application of production sharing was strongly resisted by the oil companies, not only by the majors but also by others who were not attracted by the notion of putting capital into an enterprise which they were not allowed to own or manage. The US government of the time supported the majors in their opposition. The new contracts were certainly less favourable to foreign oil companies than the existing work contracts. However, not only did the PSC eventually become the dominant form of arrangement in Indonesia but it was soon being imitated elsewhere. By the 1980s, the concept of production sharing for oil and gas had been adopted into the petroleum legislation of many other countries, such as Egypt, Chile, Malaysia, Philippines, Peru, Sudan, Libya, Syria, Jordan, China, Russia, Angola and Bangladesh.[10] Production-sharing contracts as in Indonesia are usually entered into with the state oil company although the government is in reality the other partner. This is meant to give a greater degree of control over the operation of the private contractor; in reality the foreign firm often manages and operates the oilfield directly.

Two oil production-sharing contracts were signed in Indonesia in 1961 with two minor companies, Asamera and Refican and there had been an earlier, oil for financial and technical assistance, arrangement with a Japanese group. But these were not very important. The first significant production-sharing contract which was to form the basis for subsequent agreements with foreign oil companies was signed in 1966 between Permina and a consortium of US interests known as IIAPCO (the Independent Indonesian American Petroleum Company).[11] In May 1967 the US independent, Continental Oil (Conoco), became the first of the major companies to sign a production-sharing contract for acreage in south east Kalimantan. Subsequently, in the same year, two other major US independents, Union Oil and Sinclair Oil signed a PSC as partners to cover areas in north Sumatra and east Kalimantan.

Terms for production sharing have varied over the years, particularly after 1976, but the basic principles remained as first spelled out in a presidential statement of 1962. They reflected the nationalistic policy favoured by the Sukarno regime which was not prepared to accept any equity investment in the Indonesian economy. The concept of production sharing was thus envisaged as an association between a foreign source of finance and an Indonesian investor for the establishment of a specific project. It was not a joint venture as the enterprise was to be owned, managed and operated entirely by Indonesian nationals and there was to be no financial payment to foreign creditors. The foreign company was seen as just a contractor who provided services. The sovereignty of the country and of its hydrocarbon resources was recognized as sacrosanct.

The various PSCs that have been in use since 1966 have used different terms and titles, but they remain the pre-eminent legal form for the exploration and production of oil, gas and geothermal resources.

The production-sharing contract, unlike the work contract, does not divide the profit out of market proceeds to give a 'tax' payment. Instead it divides physical production, after allowing a portion of production to be retained for the recovery of pre-production and production costs. The other major differences with the contract of work are that costs under the PSC can be recovered only with production, although this is also true of a concession arrangement, and management control is in the hands of the state enterprise. Other more subtle but significant differences are that, under the contract of work there could be disagreement between government and contractor over the market prices which form the basis for computing profits. In the PSC there is, instead, a source of disagreement in the computation of cost which is the basis for determining the volume of 'profit oil'; that is the volume of production remaining after costs in the form of oil have been deducted. In the contract of work, the profit share was a fiscal concept which determined the amount of taxes to be paid to the government. In the PSCs, signed before 1976, the contractor paid no direct taxes in as much as the contractor's share of 'profit oil' was net of taxes.

Another difference between contracts of work and the production-sharing contract is in the way the pro rata domestic allocation of crude production (Domestic Marketing Obligation or DMO) is made. Under the contract of work the company's share was calculated from total production. Thus, the company would be compensated for its costs in producing the DMO plus a fee. In the PSC, however, the company's share is calculated out of its own share of production. As a result the company only receives a fee for the DMO.

The contrasts between the production-sharing contract and the concession system were also more marked than was the case with the contract of work. The concession system basically gives all production to the concessionaire and obtains all revenue from royalty and tax. Oil is owned by the country whilst still in the ground but it becomes the property of the company at the wellhead. The work contracts had already shifted the balance of ownership from the foreign companies to the host country with the principle that sovereignty over natural resources is vested in the state until the point of sale. Under the PSCs all production, including crude stored at export terminals is the property of the government with the state company as its agent. The practical impact of this in both the contract of work and the production-sharing contract is that the host country could deny sales or exports.

These new arrangements distinguished Indonesia from its fellow members of OPEC. The latter were still, in the 1960s and later, generally using the old concession system in one form or another – the exceptions being Iran and Venezuela which had already expropriated the international companies' operations in their countries.

The new arrangements under the Indonesian PSCs made royalty and posted prices irrelevant and costs were only recoverable on production. The contractor bore all the risk, which in the case of many of the new potentially oil-bearing areas in Indonesia could be very substantial.

In practice, of course, the return to the government can be adjusted to any level by changing the amount of 'profit oil' left to the contractor and its combination with any taxes subsequently levied on this 'profit oil'. Thus, despite the legal distinctions between the various forms of agreements used for encouraging and regulating exploration and development, eventually the practical commercial effects tend to be the same. Furthermore, the degree of competition and the world competitiveness of the oil, influence both companies and government in their bargaining and tend to be reflected in the contracts. At the end of the day, agreements are unlikely to have terms regarding risks and returns that are very different from those which companies can conclude in another country.

Under the PSC, a work programme with minimum exploration conditions, normally for a six- to ten-year period is agreed. The contractor usually finances all the exploration, development and production operations, just as he would under a concession arrangement. Clearly, as the contractor bears all the loss if no commercial oil is produced, he has a very strong economic interest in developing any oil deposits that are found. This is the only way in which costs can be recovered. Amortized exploration and capital expenditure and current production costs are now offset against commercial production with all expenses refunded through the entitlement to take oil. This was originally limited to a ceiling of 40 per cent of production although it has subsequently been increased. The purpose of the 40 per cent ceiling on cost recovery was, according to the former Minister of Mines, Dr Sadli, to suppress the cost of oil and hence improve the revenue for the government when the price of oil was less than $2 per barrel. However, this ability to write off up to 40 per cent of returns as costs was seen as giving an extra windfall when prices rose with the first 'oil shock'.

Indonesian oilfields generally have a short production life and a high priority has to be given to the recovery of exploration expenditures if contract terms are to be acceptable to the companies. The ability to recover the bulk of costs within the first five years under PSC conditions was a major factor in encouraging the return of the international companies in the late 1960s.

It is after exploration and development costs have been covered that the balance of production is shared in agreed proportions. The amount of oil to be retained by the contractor to cover costs was calculated originally on a basis of $5 per barrel, escalating with the UN index of manufacturing costs. Subsequently, in the second generation PSCs costs were calculated on standard accounting principles.

The proportions applied after deduction of oil for costs were originally 35 per cent for the contractor and 65 per cent for the state for a basic level of production. The first generation PSC was relatively simple. It is distinguished from subsequent versions especially by the arrangements under which Pertamina's share of production was deemed to include the contractor's tax obligation. Thus, in the original terms with no tax being paid by the contractor, the 35 per cent share of production was considered as 'clean' after tax income. This was revised in subsequent versions of the PSC and the contractual partner has to pay 56 per cent tax on its share of crude in the pre-1984 contracts and a 48 per cent tax in subsequent contracts. However, as explained below, the contractor's share of 'profit oil' is grossed up to offset the effect of the government's corporate and dividend taxes.

A major advantage of the PSC to the government is that the division of the 'profit oil' element provides a guarantee of a minimum payment to the state company irrespective of profitability or market price of oil. The state company receives revenue[12] as long as production takes place, which makes for some stability of income, and all costs are borne by the contractor until successful production is achieved. This is not so dissimilar in practice to equity oil arrangements.

With the dramatic increase in international oil prices in 1973 and 1974, the Indonesian government insisted that the resultant 'windfall' profits should be taken largely for the benefit of the state. As a result, early in 1974 companies with PSCs had their contracts revised. The contractor's equity share was valued on a base price of $5 per barrel escalating proportionately with increasing oil prices. The balance between the actual price and the base price applied to the contractor's equity was then split 85/15 in favour of the government. Subsequently, the additional revenues needed to service the substantial debts incurred by Pertamina led to a further renegotiation of contracts. These negotiations were also probably, in part, a reflection of a growing degree of interest by contractors in certain areas in Indonesia at that time. This is shown by the increase in the number of wells drilled in the early 1970s (see Figure 2.2). Difficult and protracted negotiations took place during 1975 and 1976. Finally the companies agreed to Pertamina's share of the whole balance of oil production, after deduction of costs, being increased from 65 per cent to 85 per cent as well as to some other changes. Subsequently, the production-sharing ratio in contracts was raised on a sliding scale according to output and price. Cost was in future to be calculated using accepted accounting

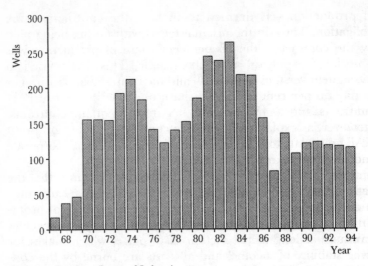

Source: *Petroleum Report of Indonesia*

**Figure 2.2** Indonesian Exploration Wells Drilled 1967 to 1994

principles but without a ceiling. This gave a useful boost to development in difficult areas by allowing 100 per cent cost recovery.

Alterations had also been made to the contracts of work early in 1974 to increase the profit share going to government. Surcharges were then added from January 1976. At that time a complication arose because of a US Internal Revenue Service ruling on 7 May, 1976 to the effect that a foreign tax credit to a US oil company for the share of production retained by the state be disallowed. Such a payment was deemed a royalty and thus not eligible as a foreign tax credit. The ruling had serious implications and meant that the Indonesian government had to redefine its cost recovery principles and modify its tax methods if US companies were to be able to claim US income tax exemptions. Under the original PSCs, income tax payments were made by the state oil company to the government on behalf of the contractor. Such payments were made out of the state company's share of 'profit oil'. This was replaced under the 1976 revisions to the PSCs by the contractor paying a portion of the 'profit oil' directly to the Indonesian government rather than to the state oil company. To accommodate the IRS ruling, the contractor's share of oil was grossed up to take into account the prevailing Indonesian tax rate. This mechanism did, however, require the setting of acceptable and clear oil prices which was done through the so-called Government Selling Price (GSP). This set off a running conflict between the government and the contractors which was only resolved in 1989 with the introduction of a realized market price formula.[13]

All oil sales to third parties were originally valued at the net realized price, that is f.o.b. Indonesia, received by the foreign company. However if Pertamina is able to obtain a better price, that would be used. Sales to affiliates of the contractor are valued on the basis of prices received on third-party sales by either party to the contract. These provisions provide some safeguard against underpricing by the foreign oil company with Pertamina having the option to take its share in the form of oil. In practice actual physical division of the oil need not take place.

In April 1989, the existing GSP was replaced by an Indonesian Crude Price formula (ICP). This formula is based on a basket of spot prices and applies to the PSCs for internal transfers, cost recovery and tax calculations as well as for sales (see Chapter 6).

The production-sharing contracts also specify signature bonus and a bonus to be paid to Pertamina when production reaches a specified level. As mentioned earlier, producers are obliged to provide a percentage of production at an agreed, very low, price to Pertamina. This, Domestic Market Obligation, is taken from the contractor's share of 'profit oil' and, depending on prevailing market conditions, may represent around 8.5 per cent of total production. This increases the split in a standard field to 90/10 in favour of the government. Contractors also have to relinquish a specified percentage of acreage over time but if an area is declared commercial the contract normally runs for 30 years from the date of signing.

Later production-sharing contracts have required the foreign company to agree to sell a certain portion of its production to local Indonesian participants as soon as production commences. This sort of local 'participation' requirement allows further financial benefits for Indonesian interests without corresponding financial risks as the participation is of a highly selective kind.

The basic structure of the PSC is summarized below:

Management:
:   Pertamina is responsible for management of operations. The contractor is the operator, responsible to Pertamina for operations in accordance with agreed work programmes.

Finance:
:   The contractor provides all financial and technical assistance for petroleum operations, and carries the risk of operating costs.

Duration:
:   The contract allows 6 to 10 years for exploration and 30 years in total if commercial production is established.

Work Programme:
:   The contractor prepares annually a work programme and budget of operating costs to be agreed with Pertamina.

Ownership of Assests:
:   All equipment purchased by the contractor becomes the property of Pertamina when landed in Indonesia. Leased equipment is exempt.

Data:
:   Pertamina has title to all data obtained from the operation.

Split:
:   Remaining production after recovery of costs is shared between Pertamina and the contractor in the proportions specified in the particular contract.

Tax:
:   The contractor pays Indonesian taxes on income. This income is the contractor's share of 'profit oil' grossed up with the prevailing Indonesian tax rate (e.g. 25 per cent share with a 48 per cent tax rate becomes a share of 28.8462 per cent). Pertamina reimburses the contractor for other taxes paid in conducting operations.

Domestic Market Obligations:
:   The contractor is to supply Indonesia's domestic requirement for crude oil (the Domestic Market Obligation, DMO) to a maximum specified. This varies but could be up to 25 per cent of the pre-tax share of 'profit oil'. Originally the fee was a low $0.20 per barrel but is currently 15 per cent of the export price. The incentives package of 1988 valued the DMO at export prices for five years.

Participation:
:   10 per cent undivided interest is to be offered to Pertamina or an Indonesian entity when

petroleum can be produced commercially. The contractor is reimbursed with 10 per cent of production costs either by a transfer out of the amounts involved or by a 'payment out of production'.

Ring Fencing: A contractor with more than one working area in Indonesia cannot consolidate financial results for calculating the obligation to the government.

Source: Barrows Co. Inc. presentation at a conference on 28 April, 1993 in Houston, Texas

An example of the way in which profits are shared and entitlements received under a production-sharing contract is shown in Table 2.3.

There obviously has to be close monitoring of the financial transactions of the companies involved in the PSCs. This assumes a high level of sophistication and expertise on the side of the monitoring authority, which has generally not been available to Pertamina in the past. Overseeing responsibilities now rests with another organization, the Foreign Contractors Management Body (BPPKA). The BPPKA reviews contractors' budgets, annual work programmes and recommendations for awarding contracts on projects once a foreign or local company has signed an agreement with Pertamina. BPPKA must also agree regarding the commercial viability of oil and gas disoveries. Pertamina's exploration and development division also supervises some foreign and local companies which have different contractual arrangements.

As a result of declining interest and reduced activity by foreign oil companies and to counter lower international oil prices, two additional modifications to the production-sharing contracts were announced in 1988 and 1989. Thus, a third generation of PSCs was brought in. These introduced more flexibility into the terms where the costs of bringing fields into production are a higher than usual proportion of total investment expenditures. They included the application of variable production-sharing ratios so that investment in frontier areas could be rewarded with an increased share of output. The government take for small fields in conventional areas was reduced to 80 per cent and in frontier areas to 75 per cent. These new measures made

**Table 2.3:**  Profit Sharing and Entitlement under a Production-Sharing Contract

|  | Barrels | Dollars |
|---|---|---|
| Production | 1,000 | 17,000 |
| Recoverable Costs | 353 | 6,001 |
| Operating Income | 647 | 10,999 |
| DMO | 72 | 1,224 |
| DMO Fee to Contractor | - | -122 |
| Government/Pertamina Share | 460 | 7,820 |
| Tax | - | 997 |
| Total | 532 | 9,919 |
| Contractor's Share | 187 | 3,179 |
| Less DMO | -72 | -1,224 |
| DMO Fee | - | 122 |
| Tax | - | -997 |
| Total | 115 | 1,080 |

|  | Entitlement to Lift | Share of Operating Income: |
|---|---|---|
| Government/Pertamina | 468[a] | 90.2 per cent |
| Contractor | 532[b] | 9.8 per cent |

Thus a normal 15 per cent 'profit' share for the contractor becomes, in this example, an actual 9.8 per cent 'profit' share

ASSUMPTIONS

Production: 1,000 Barrels

Recoverable Costs: (Production cost of $6 per barrel 1,000 barrels divided by ICP) = 353 barrels

Contractor's before tax share of operating income at 48 per cent tax rate: 28.8462 per cent (on 85/15)

Domestic Market Obligation (DMO) 7.2 per cent of all production. (25 per cent of pre-tax share of production)

DMO fee paid to contractor by Pertamina. $1.70 per barrel (i.e. 10 per cent of export price)

Assumed Indonesian crude price (ICP): $17 per barrel.

a.    PSC Share Plus DMO
b.    Recoverable Cost Oil Plus PSC Share Less DMO

a significant contribution to restoring the oil companies' confidence in investing in Indonesia. However, one feature, designed to solve the issue of commerciality in small fields in the early stage of production did not prove popular. This involved setting aside a first tranche of production to be shared between government and contractor before cost recovery; thus giving a 'floor' for government revenue and a guaranteed income from fields where costs may absorb the bulk of returns. This had no effect on companies already producing and has not been enforced for existing PSCs. It is, however, still a part of the current package.

On 31 August, 1992 additional new incentives were introduced, retroactively to 1 January, to encourage oil and gas development. This was a further package within four years designed mainly to encourage more exploration in less accessible regions which may have been considered uneconomic by the industry. It provides marginal additional incentives for the development of gas fields and for oil in high risk 'frontier' areas, but was not enough to stimulate much new activity.

New contracts for gas exploration in conventional areas will provide the contractor with 35 per cent of production instead of the former 30 per cent. For frontier areas, the share of gas produced that goes to the contractor is increased to 40 per cent. At the same time, the incremental share system for oil in frontier areas was replaced by a straight 80/20 split. For offshore drilling at depths of more than 1,500 metres the split will be 70/30 for oil and 55/45 for gas. The new packages also increased the price of the oil that the contractors are obliged to provide for the domestic market to 15 per cent of the export price, as compared with 10 per cent previously. In addition there are changes to depreciation allowances, with an acceleration of the past terms to half of the asset's useful life. Investment credits and the overall exploration incentives for gas fields were brought into line with those for oil. These moves were in response to the general feeling that previous terms were too heavily weighted against the contractors for most new areas.

The first PSC to include all the incentives introduced in August 1992 was signed with the US independent company Arco on 27 February, 1993 for a block on Irian Jaya. The last two surviving contracts of work were converted to PSCs during 1993. PSCs are the dominant form of contractual arrangement although they cover a variety of different terms depending on when they were signed. In 1992, PSCs were responsible for 96 per cent of all crude oil produced in Indonesia.

In January 1994, the government introduced a fourth package

of incentives for oil in specific frontier areas in response to declining activity. This improved the after tax oil split between Pertamina and the contractor to 65/35 for frontier areas and in deepwater areas of more than 1,500 metres depth. Previously the split was 80/20. The split for gas after this package remains at 60/40. It also provides a higher price for the domestic market obligation; it is now 25 per cent of official prices for the new contracts compared with 15 per cent under the third package. There is, in addition, a cut in the proportion of production taken as first tranche from 20 to 15 per cent. These measures more than compensate for the loss in investment credit that was a part of the package. The government's belief is that these incentives will attract new investors to the high risk and remote areas. Taken with the whole of the third generation of contracts, it is hoped that the new measures will enable production to be maintained at 1 mb/d for the next 25 years and that the onset of net oil imports can be delayed until at least 2010.

Pertamina has awarded PSCs of this kind in a number of unexplored areas but the few discoveries made have tended to be small or too remote from existing pipelines to be economic. It is too early to see whether the new terms will provide the required stimulus. The main contract terms may still not be fully competitive for new exploration areas in complex geological structures or deep offshore.

The bulk of gas for liquefaction is also produced under production-sharing agreements similar to the original ones for oil. There are some differences as the foreign company is entitled to recover not only its exploration costs but its capital investment, in the form of a portion of the gas produced. The balance of gas production has until recently been divided between government and company in the ratio of 70 per cent to 30 per cent. However unlike the earlier oil contracts, but in line with the later ones, there is no ceiling on the ratio of cost recovery to total production. The government is consequently not guaranteed a minimum payment from the commencement of production. These concessions were considered necessary to induce companies to incur the high capital investment needed to start up gas developments.

An indication of the main milestones on the route towards national control of the oil producing industry is shown below:

1907:           Introduction of general mining legislation. Colonial concession system.

1945:           Independence declared. Constitution reaffirms state control over natural resources.

1945 to 1960:  Status quo. 'Let alone' agreements.

1957:           The army takes over the North Sumatran fields. Ibnu Sutowo's concept of production sharing.

1960:           Oil Mining Law No. 44. Concession rights revoked. Pertamina formed.

1963:           Contracts of work signed.

1966:           First major PSC (the first generation) signed and international recognition achieved.

1971:           Law 8 giving Pertamina exclusive rights to carry out exploration and production.

1976:           Revisions to the PSC (the second generation). Pertamina share increased to 85 per cent.

1988/89:        Further revisions to the PSC (the third generation) introducing more flexibility and reductions in Pertamina's share.

1992:           New incentives introduced to third generation PSCs and further reductions in Pertamina's share.

1993:           Last contract of work converted to PSC.

1994:           Additional incentive package for PSCs (fourth since 1988).

*Joint Venture and other Agreements.* As an additional basis for foreign investment in oil and gas development, a new form of joint-venture agreement was introduced in 1977. These joint operation agreements (JOA) were brought in for the development of the onshore areas previously reserved exclusively for Pertamina at a time when the company was in grave financial difficulties. The JOAs are designed with the intention of reducing Pertamina's own exploration costs, particularly in areas where it lacks the financial resources to develop reserves adequately. At the same time they are intended to provide the foreign companies with access to low-risk areas in which they had shown interest and previously been excluded from. Under these joint arrangements, the foreign company still has to carry all expenses for the first three years of exploration after which costs are divided on a 50/50 basis. Oil production is divided equally and the company's share further divided on the basis of the standard production contract terms. This kind of arrangement would seem to be an example of the Indonesian government edging close to an equity sharing arrangement when the need arises.

There is now also a host of other contractual arrangements in addition to the PSCs and JOAs already mentioned. These are mainly directed at encouraging exploration and development in marginal areas on Pertamina acreage. They are usually where there is little exploration risk so that the full PSC would not really be appropriate. They include Technical Evaluation Agreements (TEA), Technical Assistance Contracts (TAC), Joint Operating Bodies (JOB), Enhanced Oil Recovery Contracts (EOR) and Loan Agreements (LA).

The EOR contract was introduced in 1987 as a move to relieve Pertamina of some of the burden of maintaining old productive fields. It is aimed at encouraging the involvement of qualified foreign firms in using enhanced oil recovery techniques under production-sharing contracts instead of service contracts. Cost recovery is from up to 65 per cent of the value of the contractor's share of the incremental oil production achieved through the application of EOR techniques.

TEAs allow oil companies access to Pertamina data for areas not yet available as a PSC working area. This agreement is basically an option that allows international companies to conduct seismic surveys or geological studies in open acreages. It is a way of acquiring additional knowledge of an area before it is offered for exploration under a PSC. There is a requirement to undertake additional exploration work with a corresponding right of refusal when the acreage is let.

The loan agreements were made with the Indonesian Nippon Oil Corporation and Java Oil to provide loan facilities for Pertamina to conduct exploration. If discoveries are made, the lenders will be compensated with crude oil in accordance with an agreed formula.

In the late 1960s, when faced with budgetary problems, Pertamina began offering international companies the right to drill deeper layers in its own producing fields under the TAC. Needless to say, all financing is provided by the contractor. These agreements, where the contractor takes over an existing Pertamina field and takes a share of production over a certain level, have been increasing recently. The other arrangements are mainly applicable to the development of marginal areas.

Major international companies have not often availed themselves of these models but independents and local companies have shown considerable interest.

There are special terms involved in contracts for exploration in the area of the Timor Gap that is currently disputed with Australia. This is an area which is considered to be rich in hydrocarbon potential. The contract terms, which were agreed in February 1991 as part of the Timor Gap Treaty, are designed to recognize the divided nature of the area. The Joint Authority's share of liftings in the area to be developed by both countries is to be split 50/50 between Australia and Indonesia with a formula to avoid double taxation on the contractor's business profits. The other two areas covered by the Treaty are to be developed by Indonesia and Australia individually but with a fairly modest tax payment being made to the non-involved country when production occurs. The contracts include a first tranche of 10 per cent of production to the government concerned but thereafter production is split on a 50/50 basis. By early 1992, 11 PSCs covering the joint area had been signed involving a total investment of $362 million and covering the drilling of 45 exploration wells. The first of these wells was drilled by the US independent company Marathon late in 1992. The level of activity indicated by this investment should be seen against a total expenditure for Indonesia on exploration and development of $1.3 billion in 1992.

The existing 120 sites covered by working agreements in 1993 comprised 87 standard PSCs, 21 JOAs, 7 EORs, 3 TACs as well as 2 contracts of work. The number of PSCs increased at an uneven rate but reached record levels in the early 1980s. As mentioned, the contractual revisions of 1976 and 1977, the second generation of PSCs, took place against the background of a major financial crisis in Indonesia involving substantial foreign debts accumulated by Pertamina. During the Pertamina crisis, foreign investment in hydrocarbons fell but rose to high levels in the early 1980s. By 1983, over 60 PSCs were in force and Indonesia's terms were considered more attractive than those currently available in some other countries. However, weakening international markets for oil caused a slowdown in the signing of contracts which slumped from an average of ten per year in the late 1970s to an annual average of only two during the four years to 1986. There has, however, been something of a recovery since then in response to the government's economic liberalization and greater flexibility on terms. From seven contracts in 1987 the number signed rose to a peak of 19 in 1991 together with four extensions. All but one of the 1991 signings were with non-Indonesian companies. However, only 11 contracts were signed in 1992 and 19 were relinquished. It is believed that 13 new PSCs were signed in 1993. Up to November 1994 only one new PSC had been signed together with three TACs. At the beginning of 1994 there were 115 active contracts, only a modest increase over the 107 active at the beginning of 1993. In 1993, 117 wells were drilled, of which 73 were wildcats and the rest appraisals. There were some 20 discoveries. All but seven of the exploration wells were drilled in western areas under contracts already supporting commercial production. It is hoped that the fourth package of incentives introduced in January 1994 will attract more activity and bring the number of wells drilled back towards the peak of over 260 reached in the early 1980s.

*Conclusions.* Much more seems likely to be necessary if crude oil exports are to be maintained at reasonable levels. If current activity does not succeed in proving up large volumes of oil soon one option must be to increase the incentives for secondary and tertiary recovery in mature fields. This would mean more emphasis in future on the EOR type of contract or a model derived from the other arrangements available or substantial changes to the current PSC. One suggestion is to change the present 'ring fence' prohibition against allowing exploration expenditures in non-producing PSC areas to be offset against revenues in producing contract areas.

In recent years, government policy seems to have been to sign a large number of agreements with minor and relatively unknown companies. This was also, in part, forced on the government by the lack of interest from the major oil companies who have in the past been somewhat wary of investing in Indonesia under the terms available. This policy was, perhaps, not conducive to a broad and sustained development of oil and gas reserves and may now be shifting slightly towards trying to attract major oil players.

The Indonesian government has always sought to negotiate contracts that satisfy its political imperative of being seen to assert its sovereign rights over oil and gas. Indeed it achieved full control over oil and gas through its hydrocarbon laws long before many other major, and more vocal, producers.

At the same time as achieving full national control, Indonesia has had to meet the other more down to earth imperative of ensuring an adequate supply of oil and gas. It has had to go along with the reality of attracting investment and expertise from foreign companies increasingly faced with opportunities elsewhere. Whilst still keeping more or less within the political confines of the original Oil Act, it would seem from the range of terms now available, that pragmatism and innovation in attracting investment for oil and gas development have been increasing over the years.

It is not clear whether Indonesia is prepared to go further than the 1992 and 1994 packages to stimulate increased activity and to adjust unpopular measures. The government may continue, as in the past, with an approach of just reacting when it perceives that a lack of outside interest is having a serious effect on development and then clawing back what it can when the situation is apparently improving. Certainly, there now seems to be a more sensitive response to the 'market'.

Changing conditions and perceptions in international oil and gas markets and particularly the many opportunities for up-stream investment outside of Indonesia perhaps necessitate another innovative approach on contractual terms. Something has to be done to stimulate more activity, particularly in Eastern Indonesia.

## The Development of Oil Production

The outside view of the petroleum legislation in place in Indonesia and the perception of volumes available to be recovered, must ultimately find a reflection in the level of exploration and development activity. Such activity needs to continue at a high rate simply to maintain current production levels against a background of difficult geology, small fields and remote terrain.

Crude oil production increased rapidly through most of the

1970s. The total volume of oil production exceeded 1 mb/d for the first time in 1972 and reached a peak of 1.686 mb/d in 1977. Production declined thereafter and stagnated through the 1980s although it has increased slightly in recent years (see Figure 2.1). 1991 was a good year with increasing output from new fields finding export markets and total crude and condensate production increased by 9 per cent in 1991 to an average 1.6 mb/d. This was the country's highest production rate in a decade and close to the all-time production record of 1977. Regaining the peak, however, has proved elusive; production fell by 6 per cent in 1992 and by a further 1 to 2 per cent in 1993 and is currently running at just under 1.5 mb/d.[14] Output could probably be boosted to a little over 1.7 mb/d, including 0.2 of condensates, on a short-term basis.

There are well over 300 fields producing oil. They are located in all the main islands of the archipelago as well as in the offshore areas but the bulk of production still comes from long established areas in Sumatra.

Indonesia is mainly characterized by many small but numerous fields requiring a large number of wells to be drilled in relation to oil produced. Generally production ranges from a few hundred to a few thousand b/d. There is some mitigation in that fields are usually shallow, with many less than 3,000 ft. and some at 300 ft. Production curves are often bell shaped and the decline rate high with fields being exhausted within 7 to 15 years. As a result of these characteristics, exploration has to be maintained at a high rate to compensate for the decline of existing fields.

There are only 28 fields that have a production of 10,000 b/d or more but these together make around 80 per cent of total production. Thus the remaining fields, some 300, are responsible for only 20 per cent of total production, representing an average production per field of just under 1,300 b/d. Details of the major fields are shown in Table 2.4.

If a major field is defined as one with a cumulative production of over 100 mb or as a field producing more than 20,000 b/d, then Indonesia has 25. Many of these are now played out but, of the current major fields, seven are offshore and all the major discoveries of the 1980s have been in offshore areas.

Although there are gas condensates and lighter crudes,

**Table 2.4**: The Major Oilfields of Indonesia

| Field | Year Discovered | API Gravity 1993 | Average Crude Oil Production 000 Barrels Per Day 31 December, 1992 | Cumulative Production Million Barrels |
|---|---|---|---|---|
| Minas | 1944 | 35.0 | 211 | 3,681 |
| Duri | 1941 | 22.0 | 197 | 727 |
| Arun | 1971 | 55.0 | 106 | 510 |
| Ardjuna | 1969 | 37.0 | 97 | 826 |
| Widuri | 1988[a] | 24.0 | 70 | 81 |
| Handil | 1974[a] | 33.0 | 44 | 734 |
| Attaka | 1970[a] | 32.0-42.0 | 38 | 537 |
| Cinta | 1970[a] | 34.0 | 15 | 196 |
| Nilam | 1974 | 33.4 | 55 | 58 |
| Badak | 1972 | 34.4 | 15 | 105 |
| Kakap | 1980[a] | 43.0-51.0 | 16 | 46 |
| Seppingan | 1973[a] | 25.0-38.0 | 34 | 73 |
| Walio | 1973 | 34.3 | 10 | 169 |
| Intan | 1987 | 32.0 | 18 | 37 |
| Petani | 1964 | 33.0-35.0 | 11 | 290 |
| Libo | 1968 | 35.0 | 13 | 12 |
| Jene | 1985 | 35.0 | 10 | 37 |
| Nilam | 1974 | 33.4 | 15 | 58 |
| Semberan | 1974 | 30.0 | 10 | 4 |
| Bekasap | 1955 | 34.0 | 18 | 432 |
| Bangko | 1970 | 34.0 | 30 | 387 |
| Pedada | 1973 | 33.0 | 10 | 85 |
| Balam | 1969 | 29.0-33.0 | 13 | 121 |
| Zamrud | 1975 | 40.0 | 16 | 91 |
| Beruk | 1974 | 38.0-40.0 | 10 | 67 |
| Butun | 1982 | 44.0 | 11 | 19 |
| Kotabatak | 1952 | 29.0 | 19 | 166 |
| Belida etc. | 1989[a] | 39.0-47.4 | 77 | 2 |
| Total | | | 1,174 | 9,188 |
| All Other Fields | | | 396 | 5,887 |
| Total Indonesia | | | 1,505 | 15,380 |

a. Offshore Field

Sources of basic data: *Oil and Gas Journal*, 26 December, 1994; *International Petroleum Encyclopedia*, 1993

Indonesian crude is typically of medium gravity with a paraffin base and has a moderate to high pour point, a low sulphur content and a relatively low gas to oil ratio. Unfortunately, new fields tend increasingly to have heavier and less valuable crude oil grades.

Indonesian oil is always said to be expensive to produce although it has freight advantages for the South East Asian market that help to compensate. Detailed data on costs per barrel are calculated by the contractors and submitted to Pertamina in accordance with the contract provisions. Such data is naturally, commercially sensitive and not publicly available. On a basis of total expenditure on exploration and development and production between 1988 and 1992, the average 'cost' per barrel of all hydrocarbons produced has been $4. This is, of course, only a very rough indication. The substantial proportion of crude oil produced through steam injection and other artificial lift methods, the low level of well productivity and the short life of many fields would certainly indicate a fairly high average cost. The cost of steam flooding elsewhere, for example, can range between $5 and $20 per barrel with investment costs of the order of $8,000 to $24,000 per barrel daily of capacity.[15] At the end of 1992 out of 8,047 producing wells nearly 90 per cent needed artificial lift to produce.

Exploration costs in the vast area of land and sea covered by Indonesia, must vary considerably with local conditions of terrain, of vegetation, water depth, distance from shore, accessibility and remoteness of site. In the remote areas exploration costs can be very high. Logistical costs are particularly high in eastern Indonesia where in some locations only helicopters can bring in men and materials. Some plugged and abandoned wells there are said to have cost as much as $30 million. The large number of farm-outs that occur are probably also an indication of a strong desire by exploration companies to limit their exposure in frontier areas that represent high technical risks and high costs.

As oil has increasingly to be squeezed out of old and difficult fields, well productivity overall has been declining since the mid-1970s (see Table 2.5). The average output per well of 174 b/d at the end of 1993 was nearly one-third of productivity in the

**Table 2.5**: Production Per Well. Barrels Per Day

| | | | | | | | |
|------|-----|------|-----|------|-----|------|-----|
| 1972 | 438 | 1978 | 453 | 1984 | 314 | 1990 | 177 |
| 1973 | 506 | 1979 | 419 | 1985 | 229 | 1991 | 206 |
| 1974 | 538 | 1980 | 418 | 1986 | 246 | 1992 | 187 |
| 1975 | 431 | 1981 | 407 | 1987 | 218 | 1993 | 174 |
| 1976 | 475 | 1982 | 319 | 1988 | 196 | | |
| 1977 | 494 | 1983 | 271 | 1989 | 202 | | |

Sources: *The Petroleum Resources of Indonesia* and *Oil and Gas Journal*

mid-1970s. This decline is partly a reflection of the great age of the major fields, most of which were first developed in the early 1970s or even earlier but also reflects the dearth of new major discoveries. Such output levels are still a long way from that of the played out fields of the USA, for example, where production is only 12 b/d per well. However, it contrasts dramatically with more than 1,000 b/d per well in Malaysia and over 2,000 b/d per well in the UK North Sea.[16] This kind of contrast, in the context of the terms offered for exploration and development, has a significant bearing on decisions made on whether to invest in one country or another.

The potential for large new discoveries of fields with half a billion barrels or more would seem to be low. Since the discovery of the Belida field in 1989, no fields have been discovered that have more than 100 mb of proved reserves.[17] It is said that further discoveries are more likely to be in the low of the range 50 to 200 mb but there may well be pleasant surprises in some of the underexplored areas of eastern Indonesia and elsewhere. Since oil was first produced in the 1890s, at least one major field has been discovered almost every decade. The exceptions were in the 1910s and, as yet, in the 1990s.

Minas is by far the largest field ever discovered in Indonesia. Although it was first drilled in Central Sumatra in 1944 it has a cumulative production of some 3.7 billion barrels. Both Minas and Duri in the prolific Rokau block are operated by the long established Caltex Pacific. Indeed, Caltex is still the major producer in Indonesia, operating 97 fields in four contract areas in Sumatra and producing around 45 per cent of the country's oil. Caltex has recently been granted an extension to operate the Rokau block to the year 2021. This should enable it to make additional investment in enhanced recovery projects; the existing steam flood operation at Duri is already the largest in the world.

Just six fields, Minas, Duri, Arun, Widuri, Ardjuna and Belida are between them responsible for 50 per cent of Indonesia's total daily production of crude oil. After the completion of the second development phase during 1994, the Belida field operated by Conoco has reached an output of around 130,000 b/d. It is now the largest producing field after Minas and Duri. The Arun field is basically a gas field producing gas for export but also substantial volumes of condensates with Mobil as the operator. Unfortunately, condensate production is declining from this field which supplies the bulk of the country's condensate. Ardjuna is an Arco field also associated with gas and Maxus Energy Inc. is the operator for the Widuri field. Production from this latter field has increased dramatically in recent years; it was producing just over 10,000 b/d in 1990 but is now running at well over 100,000 b/d.

Although Pertamina has been in existence in one form or another since the earliest days of the Republic of Indonesia and is the flagship of the national oil industry, it was only involved directly in 5 per cent of crude oil and condensates produced in 1993. As Table 2.6 illustrates, the overwhelming bulk of production is now obtained under production sharing or related contracts. Caltex still dominates production but Maxus with the Widuri field, Arco, Mobil and Conoco are major players. These four companies together with Caltex accounted for 74 per cent of the country's production of crude and NGLs in 1993.

### The Outlook for Future Production

Current oil reserves were largely built up during three periods of intensive exploration, in the 1940s, the late 1960s and the early 1980s. Output from many of the existing fields is declining; for example, production from the largest field, Minas, is expected to fall by 3 per cent in 1993. The more recently discovered Widuri field is also suffering a decline in production. On the other hand, production from the Duri field has been increasing

**Table 2.6**:   Crude Oil and NGL Production by Companies. Thousand Barrels Per Day

| Company | 1970 | 1992 | 1993 |
|---|---|---|---|
| Pertamina | 88 | 68 | 75 |
| Caltex (C. Sumatra) | 707 | - | - |
| Stanvac (C. + S. Sumatra) | 48 | 22 | - |
| Calasiatic/Topco (Sumatra) | - | 4 | - |
| Total Contracts of Work | 755 | 26 | - |
| Stanvac (C. + S. Sumatra) | - | - | 21 |
| Caltex (Riau. C. Sumatra) | - | 671 | 667 |
| ARCO (N.W. Java Sea) | - | 130 | 110 |
| Maxus (S.E. Sumatra) | - | 168 | 148 |
| Conoco (Natuna) | - | 11 | 77 |
| Unocal (E. Kalimantan) | - | 74 | 68 |
| Lasmo (Malacca Straits) | - | - | 30 |
| Hudbay (Malacca Straits) | - | 37 | - |
| Total (E. Kalimantan) | - | 71 | 65 |
| Marathon (Natuna) | - | 21 | 16 |
| Mobil (N. Sumatra) | - | 112 | 107 |
| Asamera (N./S. Sumatra) | - | 24 | 22 |
| Santa Fe (Irian Jaya) | - | - | - |
| Vico (E. Kalimantan) | - | 47 | 55 |
| Others | 10 | 29 | 28 |
| Total Production Sharing etc. | 10 | 1,411 | 1,429 |
| Total Indonesia | 854 | 1,505 | 1,504 |

Sources: *OPEC Annual Statistical Bulletin*; O.J. Bee, *The Petroleum Resources of Indonesia*; *Petroleum Report of Indonesia*, 1994; *Oil and Gas Journal*, 31 January, 1994; 26 December, 1994

through the application of Enhanced Oil Recovery techniques and this is increasingly seen as a way, albeit costly, of increasing production from other old fields. Hence the special contract terms for such activity.

Exploration drilling reached a peak in 1983 with exploration expenditure running annually at an average of $1.4 billion in money of the day for each of the years between 1980 and 1985. But the low level of exploration activity in the second half of the 1980s, when wells drilled and exploration expenditure fell to one-third of the earlier peak, has diminished prospects for the next few years considerably. This fall in activity reflected the dramatic fall in international oil prices in 1986 but was also, in part, due to dissatisfaction with operating terms and conditions. Exploration expenditure increased substantially during 1990, remained around the same level for two years and increased again in 1993 (see Table 2.7). Seismic surveys in terms of area, which had set an all-time Indonesian record in 1991, fell by 29 per cent in 1992. Some 80 per cent of this seismic activity was offshore.

With the number of PSCs signed in 1992 and 1993 having dropped dramatically from 1991, it seems likely that exploration activity will not pick up over the next year or so at least. One fairly significant element is that the proportion of successful discoveries still tends to be around the level of 40 to 50 per cent common in the 1980s.[18]

The government has to pin its hopes on contractors proving up sufficient reserves to keep the country exporting substantial volumes of oil and gas well into the next century. It has tried to stimulate activity by modifying the terms of the PSCs no less than four times since 1988. The introduction of a variety of new types of arrangement to encourage additional recovery programmes and development in difficult areas may have helped. These measures are, however, still not considered by the international oil industry to be enough to stimulate the substantial additional exploration that the country needs. Oil and gas fields are tending to get smaller and much of the potential resources are in difficult areas. There are several countries which appear to have better oil prospects and conditions to attract scarce exploration funds.[19] Pertamina apparently attributes the poor level of exploration to exogenous factors, including reduced earnings by major oil companies in recent years which translated into fewer funds for exploration.

**Table 2.7**: Exploration Expenditure. US $ Million

| | | | | | |
|------|------|------|-------|------|-------|
| 1970 | 66 | 1983 | 1,481 | 1989 | 831 |
| 1975 | 458 | 1984 | 1,286 | 1990 | 1,257 |
| 1977 | 273 | 1985 | 1,177 | 1991 | 1,343 |
| 1980 | 909 | 1986 | 966 | 1992 | 1,324 |
| 1981 | 1,456 | 1987 | 583 | 1993 | 1,815 |
| 1982 | 1,723 | 1988 | 728 | | |

Source: *Petroleum Report of Indonesia*, 1994

The government has to some extent been inhibited from bolder moves in changing the terms it offers potential investors by its firm policy of national ownership and control of hydrocarbon resources, and the need to maintain the dominance and fortunes of Pertamina. A substantial acceleration of activity, particularly in the eastern areas would be helped by a perception of steadily increasing oil prices; but this does not appear to be on the horizon. Failing this, and perhaps even if oil prices were to rise, there must be more favourable contract conditions than are currently available. One proposal by existing producers is to be allowed to partially offset exploration costs in new areas against earnings from contracts that are producing elsewhere in the country, i.e. changing the 'ring fencing' condition of the PSCs. Unless some further changes are made it seems likely that many companies will continue to concentrate their efforts on those areas where risks and/or costs are relatively low.

Government policy for some years has apparently been to pursue an increased number of deals of relatively small scope with new and often minor players. Views in government circles still differ on the wisdom of using many small companies, with the more critical considering that this policy is unlikely to result in long-term sustainable production. On the face of it, such a policy does not seem an efficient way of encouraging optimal development of Indonesia's hydrocarbon resources. It does though allow considerable flexibility to be exercised on contractual terms and on targeting specific areas of activity. However, it would seem to spread the technical and administrative effort rather thinly and, in the event, does not seem able to attract the very substantial investment and technical expertise needed for optimum and sustained production.

Pertamina's claims that there is currently a new 'third wave' of exploration under way after the previous peaks in the early 1970s and early 1980s may ring a little hollow at the moment. However, the prospect is not entirely gloomy. Certainly, in 1993 there were almost 100 contractors prospecting for oil and gas in Indonesia. To date, general exploration activity has been better in the 1990s than in the late 1980s and is now at a higher level than for many years. In addition to the foregoing activity, the signing of the agreement with Australia had brought about a surge of interest in the potentially very productive Timor Gap

Zone of Cooperation. By the beginning of 1993, 11 out of the 14 blocks involved had been awarded.

The modest revival of interest in recent years is unlikely to have come from any belief in higher oil prices but is apparently due to a number of factors, most of which stem from the changes that were made to contractual conditions:

- The sale of oil produced at realistic market prices.
- Greater autonomy for contractors during the initial exploration phase.
- Improved procurement procedures.
- Better terms for marginal and higher risk exploration.
- Additional incentives for enhanced oil projects.
- Postponement of the value-added tax on certain exploration outlays.
- Perhaps indirectly for oil, from the change to negotiating gas prices between producer and consumer instead of terms being decreed by the government.
- The extension of terms for existing major producers, Caltex and Maxus.

A more fundamental reason when weighing up the merits of investment in Indonesia as opposed to the many opportunities elsewhere in the world has been the general stability of the country and the increasingly technocratic and pragmatic approach to development.

Unfortunately for the long-term building up of substantial new reserves, the direction of activity is still not focused where it might be productive. Exploration is moving only very slowly away from traditional areas. Only 8 out of 124 exploration wells completed in 1992 were in eastern Indonesia. Similarly, for 1993, only 19 out of the budgeted 207 exploration wells are in the east.

Although the first contracts awarded in the 1960s and 1970s were successful, more recent results have not been good. Of more than 130 contracts awarded since 1976, only one is thought to be both producing and making a profit. The early 1990s has already seen some reduction in representation by the international companies in Indonesia as other prospects in South East Asia and in the former Soviet Union present themselves.

There is a desperate national need to sustain and, if possible, increase crude oil production. The rate of growth in domestic

**Table 2.8:**   Exploration and Development Activity in Indonesia in 1993

| | |
|---|---|
| Number of Active Contracts | 111 |
| Number of New Contracts | 12 |
| Total Contracted Areas | 748,473 km.$^2$ |
| Exploration Wells Drilled | 114 |
| Discovery Wells Drilled | 27 (oil) |
| | 27 (gas) |
| Seismic Activity | 134 thousand km. |
| Petroleum Company Expenditures: | |
|     Exploration | $1,815 million |
|     Production | $1,243 million |
|     Others | $382 million |
|     Total | $3,440 million |

Source: *Petroleum Report of Indonesia*, 1994

oil demand is now somewhat lower than in the past and oil production is close to the levels of the peak years. Nonetheless, Indonesia could, by the turn of the century, become a net oil importer. The Minister of Mines and Energy has said that even were domestic product demand to remain flat, Indonesia would need to discover 500 mb of oil a year to maintain current export levels and a reserves to production ratio of 20 years. In practice, demand will probably still be growing at a significant pace well into the next century unless drastic measures are taken. A discovery rate of double this estimate would, we feel, be necessary to maintain exports if demand continues to grow at anywhere near past rates.

The greater use of natural gas and other domestic sources of energy to free up more oil for export as well as the expansion of gas exports is one of the answers to the problem. Another answer clearly lies in attracting much more investment, particularly interest from substantial companies with advanced technology to offer. Indonesia has been a pioneer in developing new terms to attract outside investment in the past as this chapter has attempted to show. Some further and major enhancement of the present contractual arrangements to make them more flexible and tailored to the prevailing climate in the hydrocarbon industry would seem to be needed to bring forward production at adequate levels.

One key frontier area with substantial potential for oil, as well as gas, is the Natuna Sea. Marathon, Conoco and Chevron have all made significant finds in this area and Conoco's Belida field is one of the two largest oilfields discovered in Indonesia during the last 15 years. The Director of Exploration and Production of Pertamina has said that until 1996, the potential for crude oil production will remain at 1.5 mb/d. The current five-year plan, Repelita Vl, has 1.53 mb/d of crude and condensates as its budget projection for production in 1994/95. There is a view in some quarters that production is set to fall within the next year or so, although it should be said that such pessimism has proved wrong in the past. Certainly, the low level of exploration in the mid-1980s has reduced considerably the possibility of increasing production levels through much of the rest of the 1990s. Some production increases will come over the next year or so from Caltex's enhanced oil recovery operations in the Duri field, which is expected to peak at just over 300,000 b/d by the late 1990s. The Belida field which was only discovered in 1989 is expected to peak in 1994 at around 94,000 b/d and there should be some increase from Pertamina's own operations. However, condensate production is expected to decline from the Arun field as is production from most other mature fields.

Most industry analysts, and it is believed Pertamina itself, continue to forecast a small but steady downward trend from about 1995 to the end of the decade. A fall to below 1 mb/d by the year 2000 has been mentioned, if there are no major discoveries. However, this may be unduly pessimistic given the apparent size of the resource base and the potential to attract more activity through better terms.

There is little doubt that just maintaining the production of crude and NGLs at recent levels requires a substantial effort; some 400 to 500 mb of crude oil need to be proven up each year to prevent reserves falling. This level has not been achieved in recent years. Oil reserves discovered by contractors during 1985 to 1992 averaged just over 100 mb per annum. However, over the last 20 years or so additions to reserves have averaged just over 400 mb per annum.[20] To maintain such rates of proving up new reserves under increasingly difficult conditions in what is considered by some geologists to be a maturing oil province, will certainly be difficult. It is only through major discoveries offshore and in the east that it might be achieved. It is hoped that offshore production will eventually yield perhaps two-thirds of all future discoveries, but the current level of investment and drilling does not appear adequate.

Actually to increase production to the sort of volumes required to maintain exports at levels adequate to support satisfactory economic growth represents an even more formidable task. To increase and sustain a production rate of, say, over 2 mb/d, would require the discovery of around 1 billion barrels per annum. Evidently this would have to involve a much greater degree of activity in the offshore and remoter areas than is currently envisaged. In the short to medium term, increased production is likely to be feasible only from a rapid extension of producing facilities in existing fields. Even here, there are severe constraints of reservoir pressure, well capacity and pipeline and storage facilities to be overcome.

Figure 2.3 gives an indication of a range of feasible future production levels for hydrocarbon liquids to the year 2010. The high of the range assumes a discovery rate of some 1.2 billion barrels of crude oil per annum and a recoverable resource base of around 80 billion barrels as well as an increase in natural gas

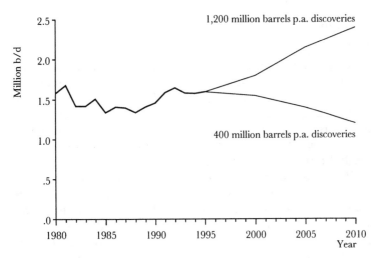

Sources:  See Figure 2.1

**Figure 2.3** Indonesian Oil Production Profiles

liquids production. In this case, production increases through to the end of the century to above 2 mb/d, which may be considered close to an upper limit of potential.

With a much lower discovery rate of 400 mb of crude oil per annum, current levels of production could be maintained for a few years. However, such a discovery rate would be inadequate to prevent an inevitable tailing off from existing reserves by the end of the century. Although this is shown as a lower case, the maintenance of production at around 1.5 mb/d through the rest of the 1990s is considered optimistic in many quarters. Some believe that a more likely profile is one where new discoveries are wholly inadequate and production declines rapidly to under 1 mb/d. Clearly, a large variety of different production profiles can be projected. Nonetheless, given the existence of a resource base of the size assumed, production levels somewhere within the lower and higher boundaries shown would be feasible. The right investment climate has to be in place but some of the pessimism may be unjustified.

The relevance of such potential levels of oil production to the economy's reliance on oil exports has to be seen in the context of the likely future growth in domestic oil demand.

## Oil Exporting Policy

*The Pattern of Crude and Condensate Exports.* The combination of declining production and rapidly increasing domestic demand for oil has led to stagnation in gross exports of crude and condensate in recent years (see Table 2.9). There are few grounds for expecting any major improvements in the near future and the export levels achieved in the 1970s seem highly unlikely to be repeated. These reached their peak in 1978 with nearly 1.3 mb/d of crude and condensate being exported.

Although the country remains a substantial net crude exporter, taking product imports and exports into account, the proportion of net exports of oil to production is steadily falling. In 1986, exports were some 67 per cent of production, while they are currently just under 50 per cent. This trend seems likely to continue.

As Table 2.10 shows, the bulk of Indonesian crude exports consists of Minas, Widuri and Duri crudes. There are also

**Table 2.9:** Gross Exports of Crude and Condensate. Thousand Barrels Per Day

|            | 1985 | 1986 | 1987 | 1988 | 1989 | 1990 | 1991 | 1992 | 1993 |
|------------|------|------|------|------|------|------|------|------|------|
| Crude      | 706  | 793  | 701  | 647  | 678  | 680  | 809  | 707  | 682  |
| Condensate | 103  | 104  | 99   | 109  | 121  | 110  | 96   | 94   | 94   |
| Total      | 809  | 897  | 800  | 756  | 799  | 790  | 905  | 801  | 776  |

Source: *Petroleum Report of Indonesia*, 1994

**Table 2.10:** Indonesian Crude and Condensate Exports in 1992

| Type | API Gravity | Company | Per Cent | Loading Source |
|------|-------------|---------|----------|----------------|
| Minas | 34° | Caltex | 30.3 | Dumai. Sumatra |
| Duri | 21° | Caltex | 14.6 | Dumai. Sumatra |
| Widuri | 33° | Maxus | 12.6 | SPM. Java Sea[a] |
| Arun (Condensate) | 54° | Mobil | 11.7 | Arun. Sumatra |
| Handil | 33° | Total | 4.1 | SBM. NE Balikpapan |
| Cinta | 33° | Maxus | 4.6 | SBM. Java Sea[a] |
| Lalang | 39° | Hudbay | 3.0 | Malacca Straits |
| Attaka | 42° | Union | 2.8 | Santan. N Balikpapan |
| Kakap | 46° | Marathon | 1.3 | Natuna |
| Badak | 41° | Huffco | 2.8 | Santan. N Balikpapan |
| Walio | 24° | Trend | 2.1 | Kasim. Between J Kasim and Iran Jaya |
| Others | | | 10.1 | |
| Total | | | 100.0 | (803 thousand barrels) |

a.    off Sumatra

Sources: *Petroleum Report of Indonesia*, 1993; *International Petroleum Encyclopedia*

substantial exports of condensate from the Arun gas field. The first two crudes are light and waxy, 34° and 33° API respectively but Duri is heavy at 20° API. Minas has dominated Indonesian crude exports for decades. Its low sulphur content of less than 0.1 per cent, has made it the ideal clean substitute for other fossil fuels in the Japanese market. Burning Minas and other Indonesian crudes directly under boilers has obviated the need for desulphurization capacity. It is, however, generally recognized as being a wasteful and less than optimum use of good quality material to employ it in such a way.

Around 58 per cent of the crude exported was part of the contractor's pre-tax entitlement, somewhat less than the 70 per cent or so of the mid-1980s. Forty per cent of crude exported represented the Indonesian government's share from the production-sharing contracts and the remainder was Pertamina's own production. The bulk of crude and condensate exports go to Pacific Rim countries, always the natural market for Indonesia's oil. Japan accounted for 53 per cent of exports in 1992. The USA was the second largest customer for Indonesian crude until very recently but its share has dropped markedly in recent years from 28 per cent of Indonesian exports in 1986 to 8 per cent in 1992. South Korea took 12 per cent of exports in 1992 and is now the second largest customer. China and Australia have also been increasing their imports in recent years of what are relatively high quality crudes. Some of the Chinese liftings may be resold to third parties although they are believed to be refining Duri and Widuri crudes. It is thought that Australia is importing substantial volumes of condensates.

The substantial fall in exports to Singapore shown in Table 2.11 reflects the reduced importance of the processing and other agreements with the Singapore refinery. They have been withering away in recent years as indigenous Indonesian refining capacity has expanded. Although all such deals were apparently cancelled briefly during 1993, overseas processing deals are

**Table 2.11**:   Exports of Indonesian Crude and Condensates by Destination. Thousand Barrels Per Day

| Destination | 1986 | 1991 | 1992 | 1993 |
|---|---|---|---|---|
| Japan | 384 | 505 | 429 | 360 |
| USA | 252 | 103 | 64 | 81 |
| South Korea | 49 | 94 | 97 | 94 |
| China | 9 | 79 | 93 | 97 |
| Australia | 21 | 65 | 58 | 57 |
| Taiwan | 20 | 43 | 39 | 43 |
| Singapore | 75 | 12 | 14 | 16 |
| Other Pacific Rim | 26 | 5 | 10 | 10 |
| Others | 60 | 0 | 0 | 18 |
| Total | 896 | 906 | 804 | 776 |

Source: *Petroleum Report of Indonesia*, 1994

reported to be running currently at some 60,000 b/d of Minas and Duri crudes. There is a return of between 40 and 45 thousand b/d of products, mainly gasoil. These deals are usually handled by traders associated with Pertamina and involve the sale of fixed volumes of crude. The proceeds are then used to buy a preset amount of products, often from unrelated sources. There are apparently no longer any counter purchase or barter oil transactions of the kind that were once popular with Pertamina.

Pertamina usually relies on affiliates and associates for its crude and product trading and there has been some criticism of the use of companies like Permindo, Perta Oil and Mindo in a middle role. It has been said that they have not kept pace with the growing competitiveness in international oil trading but the current marketing system seems unlikely to be changed in the present political climate. As long ago as 1988 it was announced by the then Oil Minister that the country planned to stop exporting crude oil and to sell only refined products. This was presumably related to the ambitious plans for the construction of new refineries. The construction of some of these new export refineries is now in abeyance. Thus it may be some years before exports of crude oil can be cut back drastically in favour of products, even if it were possible in market terms.

The increasing focus on a few major export markets for Indonesian crude seems likely to intensify through the 1990s. South East Asian countries are a natural, short haul destination for Indonesian oil exports. The demand for high quality low sulphur crudes and condensates in these markets is unlikely to abate particularly with increasing environmental pressures. Those countries with relatively prosperous and fast growing economies and energy demand, such as Japan and South Korea, will be willing and able to outbid others for Indonesian crudes. This will be particularly the case if the total export volumes available decline in future, as they may well do. However, against the background of growing demand for crude of the right quality and a potentially decreasing supply, some aspects of marketing policy do seem likely to be reassessed. This may particularly be the case for the continuation of sales of crude to Japan for under-boiler use when additional export refinery capacity finally becomes available.

Indonesia uses a mixed slate of crude oil to optimize middle distillate production in domestic refineries. As a result it has had to import increasing quantities of crude oil. Most imports are for the Cilacap refinery (see Chapter 3) which is designed to take Arabian Light and similar grades such as Iranian Light. Of the 61,000 b/d imported in 1992, most was Arabian Light crude although there were some experimental imports of Australian crudes and of a new Yemeni crude stream.

*Export Pricing Policies.* As a basis for determining the oil companies' tax and other liabilities under the production-sharing agreements it became necessary, in the 1970s, to introduce an official Government Schedule of Prices (GSP). Under this, prices have in the past indicated formal adherence to OPEC's official oil pricing structure. Official GSPs were adopted for each of the export crudes in relationship to the oil reference prices set from time to time by OPEC. Such prices were in the form of 'realized prices' rather than posted prices and were in operation long before other countries adopted such prices for settlements.[21]

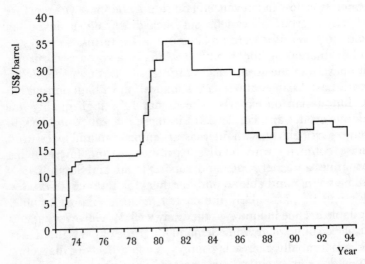

Source: *OPEC Annual Statistical Bulletin*; *Petroleum Report of Indonesia*, 1992; *Middle East Economic Survey*

**Figure 2.4** Evolution of the Official Selling Price for Minas Crude

They were, however, not necessarily the prices at which crude oil was actually sold.

The pattern of prices for Indonesian crude oil has followed in a general way those of other OPEC members. However, the government has rarely hesitated to adopt alternative measures in order to maintain or make the most of the competitiveness of its oil exports. Indeed, the prices for Indonesian crude and products have to reflect Far Eastern markets and in particular the conditions in the Japanese market. Changes to OPEC agreed prices may be useful indicators and bargaining tools but the Indonesian government can never sensibly ignore the realities of local market conditions. The price increases brought in for Indonesian crude in 1974 at the time of the 'first oil shock' were not wholly in line with those of the other OPEC countries.[22] The Indonesian government based their calculations on Indonesian oil being of better quality than Middle East oil with a different marketing catchment area for which it had an advantage in transport costs. The market realized prices are still traditionally at a premium over the international market prices for Middle East oil because of Indonesia's accessibility to the Japanese, Chinese and other Asian markets.

In October 1975 a four-level pricing system was adopted for the various Indonesian crude grades. Subsequently, at the Qatar OPEC conference of December 1976, Indonesia went along with the majority decision and revised its prices upwards by more than the Saudis. A new pricing system was adopted based on Minas crude.

Measures to improve the competitiveness of Indonesian crude over the years have included the granting of often substantial discounts to long-term Japanese customers through Pertamina's trading affiliates and the use of various tax incentives. As a result of the market upheavals that started in 1986, Pertamina adopted a highly competitive and flexible pricing policy, negotiating spot related discounts on its nominally unchanged official prices rather than entering into netback contracts. During 1987 and 1988, the government held to its official GSPs even though spot prices had fallen well below their level. Although price incentives and tax discounts were available, the government continued to claim it was adhering to the OPEC pricing line through its official prices (GSPs). These were formally retained for a few years despite ceasing to be used for the fiscal valuation of oil exported by foreign producers. This retention of the GSP was generally seen as a bargaining counter in negotiations on LNG prices which had been indexed to the official prices since 1980.

There was growing dissatisfaction amongst the production-sharing partners over oil pricing policies from 1987 onward. It was claimed that the tax incentives did not fully compensate for the revenue losses that resulted from using GSPs rather than realized prices for tax and cost recovery.[23] In response, the GSP was eventually officially withdrawn and a new pricing mechanism introduced from 1 April, 1989. The new official price mechanism, was a genuine market-related pricing scheme known as the Indonesian crude price formula (ICP) which is based wholly on spot prices. This was really a way of putting a formal gloss on what had already been taking place. The ICP applies to production-sharing contractors for internal transfers, cost recovery and for tax calculations as well as for sales.

Under the ICP, crude oil is sold at prices calculated on the basis of monthly spot prices (Asian Petroleum Pricing Index) for a basket of five internationally traded crude oils. These include two Middle Eastern crudes, Oman and Dubai, two regional crudes, Tapis and Gippsland, and the major Indonesian crude, Sumatra Light/Minas. The basket price is the arithmetic average of the mid points of the weekly price quotations from the middle of the preceding month to the middle of the current month (see Table 2.12). This makes a total of 20 prices.

Differential adjustments for each of the main Indonesian crude streams are made to the basket price calculated with prices over a 52-week period. The average of the prices for the five reference crudes for the previous 52 weeks is set against the average price for each major Indonesian crude. This 'average price' was originally derived from the Asian Petroleum Price Index (APPI). New calculations put into effect in 1992 take into account not only the APPI but also Platts and RIM. Adjustments are made to the basket price accordingly to obtain an ICP for a specific Indonesian crude. The ICPs for the lesser Indonesian grades are set at agreed differentials relating to a similar major grade.

As a result of this complicated and rather incestuous formula,

**Table 2.12:** The Indonesian Crude Price (ICP) for Sumatra Light/Minas Crude. Dollars Per Barrel

|          | *ICP* | *Spot Range*              |
|----------|-------|---------------------------|
| 8/1989   | 17.49 | 16.05-18.28               |
| 4/1990   | 17.49 | 14.97-38.43               |
| 4/1991   | 17.72 | 16.95-25.25               |
| 3/1992   | 17.35 | 17.25-17.83 (January/March) |
| 3/1993   | 18.42 | n.a.                      |

Source: *Petroleum Report of Indonesia,* 1994

the basket price lags so that when crude prices rise it is behind but, conversely, when they fall it remains above the spot market. There can be a much greater lag in changing the price differentials between crudes as the relationship between crudes is based on the previous 52 weeks. This formula is, however, reviewed every six months in order to take into account the concerns of producers and buyers.

Export sales of crude and products from Pertamina's own operations and the government's share of contractors' production are made through a number of affiliate companies of Pertamina. These companies pay Pertamina the equivalent of the ICP prices for crude oil and retain any premium that results from the sale. This arrangement causes some difficulties when there are general discounts off the ICP in markets and there appear to be moves towards direct long-term fixed price contracts with Japanese buyers particularly.

Since the ICP has been adopted there seems to have been fairly general satisfaction with the system. However, the long lag times before differentials change apparently cause problems where the relative values to customers of the individual crudes change. A significant departure from the basic pricing mechanism occurred in early 1992 when the government increased the differential for the heavy Widuri crude oil to stimulate sales. This action appears to have worked as sales subsequently picked up.

The demand for waxy crudes like Minas, Cinta and Widuri is dominated by Japanese utilities. Generally the Japanese demand for these crudes keeps the price high and out of reach of other customers. However, an unusually cool summer in 1991 caused electricity demand for air conditioning to fall and Japanese buyers became less active. As the crude sellers were forced to look for new markets Indonesian crude prices became undermined. The ICPs, based on a year's price history, continued to reflect the past strong demand from Japan long after it had weakened. This created a problem for producers and term lifters who were only able to sell cargoes on the spot market by offering huge discounts off the ICP. This led to the official change in the differential for Widuri but it took a year after the fall in Japanese demand for the ICP price to become low enough to make it competitive in other markets.

The new ICPs have made Indonesian crudes more attractive to US West Coast refiners and to the Australians. As a result, Widuri crude with the early 1992 adjustment became even more attractive and sales increased. This made it difficult for the Japanese utilities to pick up adequate supplies as their demand increases and the dominance of the Japanese market may have been weakened slightly.

Waxy, low sulphur, Minas crude together with Malaysia's light, low sulphur, Tapis crude directly and indirectly influence the pricing of all South East Asian crude oil. Demand for Minas within Indonesia is growing and revived and increasing demand from Japan in particular has at times put upward pressure on the spot prices for Minas in relation to other crudes such as Brent. However, during 1993 reduced demand from Japanese utilities for heavy sweet crude and other factors resulted in heavy discounting from ICP during the first half of 1994. These changes, in their turn, feed through to contract prices with the usual lags. There may still be a need for a slightly more flexible pricing mechanism that can adjust differentials more rapidly to changing demand patterns.

## Notes

1. A scenario drawn up by the then Senior Economic Analyst of OPEC (Al Jamadi) in 1977 quoted in O.J. Bee, *The Petroleum Resources of Indonesia*.
2. *Financial Times*, 13 May, 1993.
3. *Financial Times*, 8 December, 1994.
4. Some fairly recent estimates of oil reserves in million barrels are: *World Oil*, August 1994, 6,242 at end 1993; *Oil and Gas Journal*, 28 December,

1993, 5,779 at 1 January, 1994; Migas, 1 January, 1992, 11,300 (remaining recoverable); Petroconsultants, 7,800; A. Anderson (ex-PIW of 30 March, 1992) 6,400 (proven), 15,000 (possible).

5. Defining proven reserves as 'The estimated quantities of all liquids defined as crude oil, which geological and engineering data demonstrate with reasonable certainty to be recoverable in future years from known reserves under existing economic and operating conditions.' US EIA Annual Report 1990.

6. Estimated by the Grossling method in J.O. Bee, *The Petroleum Resources of Indonesia*, 61 to 216 billion barrels. C.D. Masters et al: World Resources of Crude Oil 20 (95 per cent), 35 (mode), 93 (5 per cent). Estimated recoverable hydrocarbon reserves quoted in *OPEC Bulletin*, September 1994 as a 'government figure' is 84.5 billion barrels of oil equivalent, with 73 per cent offshore.

7. Appointed Minister of Mines and Minister of Oil and Gas by General Suharto.

8. Sutowo was replaced as Minister of Mines in July 1966 by Ir. Bratanata who held somewhat different views on the merits of PSCs versus contracts of work. He felt that the profit sharing from the sale of oil under the latter was an adequate vehicle for obtaining just returns from Indonesian oil. He also felt that the management provisions in the contracts of work should be retained and that the way to maximize returns was to divide the oil provinces into small blocks to ensure rapid exploration and development by a large number of companies. The blocks would be put up for competitive bidding with cash bonuses on signature. His views naturally found favour with the major oil companies, not only in relation to Indonesian oil but because of their wish to avoid production sharing and loss of management control spreading to other countries. The Presidential Cabinet decided in January 1967 in favour of production sharing thus irrevocably setting the pattern for future relationships with the oil companies. O.J. Bee, *The Petroleum Resources of Indonesia*, p. 26.

9. Dr. Ibnu Sutowo opposed the work contracts as did other Indonesian officials who did not believe that they had brought any change from the old concession system. S. Carlson, *Indonesia's Oil*, p. 17.

10. It is interesting that in May 1994, the chairman of the Venezuelan state oil company PdVSA was reported as saying that it was moving towards the concept of production sharing for new acreage.

11. A small group of independent US oil men who had tried unsuccessfully in 1964 and 1965 to obtain contracts to explore for oil offshore of N.W. Java.

12. Government revenue can be seen in terms of: Pertamina's share of profit in dollars; corporation income taxes at 56 per cent of taxable income in dollars; return on the share of oil delivered for the local market. *Energy Economics*, October 1993 contains a useful article describing the incorporation of the PSCs into a decision-making model of oil production in Indonesia.

13 By the early 1980s the government had become increasingly dissatisfied with the terms of the old contracts of work. Pertamina began to

renegotiate with Caltex, insisting that the company shoulder most of the burden of OPEC's mandated reduction in Indonesia's production. A new 18-year agreement replaced the 20-year work contract that expired in 1983. This stipulated that the after-tax profit would be 88 per cent for Pertamina and 12 per cent for Caltax.

14. Much of the improvement in 1991 came from increased heavy oil production from the Widuri field. This increase in overall production was largely in response to the higher prices associated with instability in the Middle East at the beginning of the year. As Widuri production is almost entirely used as boiler fuel in the Far East, it is greatly affected by seasonal and pricing factors. Improvements in steam flood production from the Caltex Duri field also accounted for a significant share of the 1991 increase. Currently, Duri crude itself is used for generating the steam for flooding but eventually it may be possible to use Natuna gas for this purpose. Through using gas to increase secondary recovery it is said that the production capacity of the Duri field could be increased to 300,000 b/d from its present 180,000 b/d.

15. *OIES Review of Energy Costs*, 1991. Dividing annual expenditures of the companies on exploration, development and production by annual production gives a very rough indication of costs of the order of US $6.50 per barrel compared with around US $5 per barrel in 1985.

16. Not to mention over 5,000 b/d per well in the admittedly exceptional circumstances of Saudi Arabia. *International Petroleum Encyclopedia*, 1993.

17. Conoco discovered Belida in 1989 and brought it very quickly into commercial production in October 1992. It is said to have proven reserves of over 200 mb. The completion of the second phase of development in 1994 is expected to bring production to over 75,000 b/d. *Petroleum Report of Indonesia*, 1993.

18. Interestingly, gas discoveries exceeded those for oil in 1991 for the first time, but in 1992 oil discovery wells were once again more numerous (23 as opposed to 14). Ibid.

19. At the Indonesian Petroleum Association's annual dinner in October 1992, one presentation analysing rates of return available to oil companies pointed out that Indonesia's terms were lower than all other countries surveyed except for Malaysia.

20. Proven reserves are notoriously 'fluid' but on a basis of recorded reserves (from *World Oil*) having fallen between 1970 and 1992 by 1,650 mb and a cumulative production over that period of 10,752 mb, the average addition to reserves was 414 mb per annum. For the period 1980 to 1992 it was around 335 mb per annum. Total reserves of oil discovered during 1985 to 1992 totalled 723 mb according to the *Oil and Gas Journal*, 31 January, 1994. Maxus oil accounted for 38 per cent, followed by Conoco, 21 per cent and Marathon, 18 per cent. Gas reserves discovered over the same period were equivalent to 791 mb of oil.

21. In January 1963, when the companies agreed to the new contracts of work, they achieved the important concession of valuing crude oil on realized rather than posted prices. C.O. Khong, *The Politics of Oil in Indonesia*, 1986.

22. In 1974, Indonesia raised the export prices of its oil twice from $10.80 to $11.70 per barrel at the end of March 1974 and from $11.70 to $12.60 in July 1974. These increases were not in line with other OPEC countries but based on quality and marketing advantages. O.J. Bee, *The Petroleum Resources of Indonesia.*

23. Disputes over the correct price of oil were subject to a formal determining mechanism. Differences of opinion were referred to a joint price committee whose decision was binding. In the actual valuation process, however, the company could still adjust prices to suit its own particular circumstances. Discounts on the sales price could, for instance, be justified for new marketing outlets. C.O. Khong, *The Politics of Oil in Indonesia,* 1986.

# 3 THE CHALLENGE FOR DOWNSTREAM OIL: THE DOMESTIC ENERGY SCENE

## The Energy Balance and the Growth of the Markets

Whether or not Indonesia is able to maintain exports of oil in future hinges on both the levels of indigenous production that can be achieved and the future pattern and rate of growth in domestic demand for oil. This can only be considered within the context of the development of the whole domestic energy balance.

A National Energy Coordinating Board (Bakoren) was set up in November 1980 to monitor and to plan the utilization of the country's energy resources. The Board's principal aim has long been to reduce the use of oil in the domestic market and to encourage the development of other indigenous sources of energy. This has been a consistent theme of energy policy; but, with oil products currently providing the bulk of the country's demand for commercial energy, it is clear that there is still considerable scope for substitution by other fuels as well as for conservation.

There is quite a lot of energy data published from official Indonesian sources although they do not always give a consistent and cohesive picture. The abbreviated energy matrix in Table 3.1 has been prepared in an attempt to give as balanced and cohesive an indication as possible of the mixture of domestic supply sources and the pattern of national energy use.

*Exports.* As Table 3.1 indicates, Indonesia is at present a significant net exporter of oil and gas. It is also now a major coal-exporting country. Total exports of crude and products averaged over 980,000 b/d in 1992. The only major imports of energy were some 120,000 b/d of mainly Middle East crude oil for the Cilacap refinery and around 100,000 b/d of mainly middle distillate products such as diesel fuels. These product imports were more than offset by exports of 170–180,000 b/d of low sulphur waxy residue and naphtha. Coal exports have increased rapidly in recent years and are believed to have reached over 18 mt in 1994, compared with under 3 mt in 1989.

**Table 3.1:** Provisional Energy Matrix, 1992. Thousand Barrels Per Day Oil Equivalent

| | Oil | Gas | Coal | Hydro[a] | Total | Others[b] | Total Commercial |
|---|---|---|---|---|---|---|---|
| Indigenous Production | 1,593 | 962 | 294 | 58 | 2,823 | 640 | 3,463 |
| Net Exports | 771 | 576 | 202 | - | 1,549 | - | 1,549 |
| Unaccounted | +19 | - | (2) | - | +17 | - | +17 |
| Total Domestic Supply | 757 | 386 | 90 | 58 | 1,291 | 640 | 1,931 |
| Electricity Generation | 30 | 3 | 24 | 19 | | | |
| Generating Losses etc. | 71 | 7 | 50 | 39 | 167 | - | 167 |
| Electricity | | | | (76) | | | |
| LNG/Transmission and Distribution Losses | - | 216 | - | 11 | 227 | - | 227 |
| Market Demand | 643 | 160 | 16 | 65 | 884 | 640 | 1,524 |
| Transport | 263 | - | - | - | 263 | - | 263 |
| Industry | 140 | 109 | 16 | 40 | 305 | 20 | 325 |
| Residential Services | 156 | 10 | - | 25 | 191 | 620 | 811 |
| Non-Energy etc. | 40 | 26 | - | - | 65 | - | 65 |
| Refinery Use+Loss | 44 | 15 | - | - | 59 | - | 59 |

a.   Includes Geothermal
b.   Mainly Biomass
Sources: OIES database; *BP Statistical Review*; *Petroleum Report of Indonesia*, 1993

*Domestic Consumption.* Possibly around one-third of the country's total energy consumption is being met from firewood and agricultural residues at present, although in terms of end-use efficiency their effective contribution is considerably less.[1] All estimates for the consumption of such traditional fuels contain a large element of sheer guesswork, whatever the source, and Indonesia is no exception. Nonetheless, it is certain that the traditional forms of energy are still used widely not only by households for cooking but also by small industries.

In practice the continued use of biomass is not necessarily a bad thing. Outside of Java, which is mainly deforested, the land seems capable of supporting current levels of consumption on a sustainable basis. However, there is a steady and inevitable move to commercial fuels for a variety of reasons, not least of which has been the heavy subsidizing of kerosene. This substitution has placed a continuing and substantial pressure on commercial energy supplies, particularly of oil, as the economy continues to grow.

**Table 3.2:**  Percentage Shares in Commercial Primary Energy Demand.
Per Cent

|  | 1982 | 1994 |
|---|---|---|
| Oil | 86 | 58 |
| Natural Gas | 12 | 34 |
| Coal | 1 | 6 |
| Hydro/Geothermal | 1 | 2 |
| Total | 100 | 100 |

Source:  OIES database; *BP Statistical Review*

Oil currently supplies around 70 per cent (just under 60 per cent by some counts) of domestic commercial primary energy demand[2] which is a considerably lower proportion than in the early 1980s when it was over 85 per cent. Natural gas has, so far, substituted for oil in the domestic market on only a limited basis, although the process is quickening. It currently supplies 16 per cent of domestic primary energy compared with 12 per cent a decade earlier. Considerable hopes of restraining demand for oil rest on the more rapid expansion of domestic gas use in the future.

Substitution of oil by coal on the domestic market, of which there are very substantial resources, is growing, albeit rather slowly. Growth is mainly in the power sector and should become an increasingly important substitute for oil in meeting the very heavy incremental electricity requirements especially on Java. However, on even the most optimistic assumptions, coal is unlikely to increase its contribution to much above its present share of primary energy demand. Certainly it would seem unlikely to be contributing more than 10 per cent by, say, the year 2010.

There are ambitious plans to develop the country's substantial hydro and geothermal resouces as a substitute for oil in the power sector. Unfortunately, most of the economic sites on Java where the power is needed have already been exploited.

At present, each individual in Indonesia consumes on average, around 2.5 barrels of oil equivalent (boe) of commercial energy per annum. The other major exporter of hydrocarbons in South East Asia, Malaysia, has an annual income per head four times that of Indonesia and its population consumes, on average, 10 boe per capita. A fairly reasonable assumption would be that the Indonesian population will, by the year 2010, have a per capita consumption of commercial energy of at least half the level of Malaysia at present. This would mean that demand would grow at an annual average increase of some 5.3 per cent. This is below the average growth rate of the last ten years or so,[3] but would still lead to total demand for commercial energy nearly trebling to 3.3 mboe/d by 2010. Interestingly, the Director-General for Oil and Gas at the Ministry of Mines and Energy said in late-1994 that the government's target was to reduce demand growth to less than 5 per cent per annum. He expressed the view that a 3 per cent growth rate would be ideal but 'seems too low'.

The intensity with which energy is used in relation to the economy, measured in terms of boe per thousand US $ GDP, increased steadily throughout the 1970s and 1980s with industrialization and is now at around 3.7 boe per $1,000. A country's intensity of commercial energy use is roughly related to its income. The building up of basic industrialization and the spread of urbanization usually leads to a peak in intensity which is eventually followed by a decline as economies mature.[4] Interestingly, the intensity of energy use in Indonesia already appears high although in economic terms the country has a long way to go up the development curve. Intensity is slightly higher than Malaysia, 50 per cent higher than the Philippines and twice that of Thailand. Too much should not be read into such comparisons but it does seem to indicate that there is scope for improving the efficiency of energy use. Nonetheless, future demand for commercial energy is likely to be substantial under most assumptions and the upward pressure on demand for oil in the domestic market will be strong.

As Table 3.3 shows, the largest single outlet for oil products, as in almost all developing countries, is transport. 40 per cent of oil products used directly in the market are for transport purposes, largely by road vehicles. Indonesia is still on an early part of the motorization curve and vehicle growth will continue to be rapid. Indeed, over the last 15 years or so, the vehicle fleet has grown at over 15 per cent per annum. During recent years consumption of oil by power plants has grown faster than

**Table 3.3**:   Domestic Sales of Oil Products by Market in 1993

|  | *Thousand Barrels Per Day* | *Per Cent* |
|---|---|---|
| Transport | 277 | 40 |
| Industry | 153 | 22 |
| Residential etc. | 147 | 21 |
| Power Generation | 118 | 17 |
| Total | 695 | 100 |

Source: *Petroleum Report of Indonesia*, 1994

in transport.[5] However, this seems unlikely to continue as substitution of coal and gas-fuelled power stations for oil in electricity generation is well advanced. Some limitations on future growth in the transport market may be the result of traffic congestion and local pollution. Fuel efficiency is also improving in line with vehicles in the rest of the world. As a result, the growth in demand for transport fuels, mainly gasoline and diesel, may be somewhat less than the 9 per cent per annum of recent years. However, transport seems set to become the fastest growing source of oil demand during the rest of the 1990s at least. It will continue to exert major upward pressure on oil demand growth and it is a market where no real substitution by other fuels is feasible for many years. Demand for oil in this market seems likely to at least double by 2010. It is the demand for diesel fuel, largely for use in road vehicles, and to a lesser extent kerosene used in households, that has been a major cause of imbalances in the domestic supply of oil products and of the need to import crude oil.

The success of the present industrialization programme depends heavily on the replacement of small units by much larger, economic and efficient units. This should result in substantial increases in efficiency in energy use by industry. It should also mean a significant shift from the use of gasoil and kerosene to electricity, natural gas and to a minor extent coal in the industry market. The lack of investment funds is currently slowing the whole process of industrialization and substitution but future growth in demand for oil in the industry market is likely to be relatively modest.

The residential and services market represents a quarter of

domestic sales of oil. This includes the demand from small-scale commerce, shops and businesses, government buildings and hotels but is very largely the aggregation of demand by individual households for cooking and lighting. Around 7 per cent of household income is spent on fuel and power which is higher than in Pakistan, for example.

The growth of kerosene demand in the past resulted from population pressure coupled with rising incomes and substitution for non-commercial fuels. Heavily subsidized kerosene prices encouraged consumption and led to kerosene being widely used outside households for industrial purposes and for smuggling. These subsidies have been curtailed in recent years, which has led to success in reducing demand growth to well below half the annual rates of 10 per cent or so that were common a few years ago. There are also a number of other opportunities for interfuel substitution and improved efficiency in the residential and services market which could help to reduce future increases in oil demand to manageable proportions.

With overall urbanization growing at 5 per cent per annum there is an urgent need to replace kerosene with other commercial fuels. There are three small gas grids but major gas penetration requires a substantial load with a concentration of high income groups to warrant substantial investment in a high pressure system. LPG would be suitable, but at present the overwhelming bulk of production is exported.

Electricity has penetrated very rapidly into both households and industry with the expansion of public and private capacity and rural electrification programmes. Total electricity consumption has grown at an average 15 per cent per annum over the last five years, although it will be many years before the backlog of demand can be satisfied. Currently, the state-owned generator, PLN, operates some 10 GW of capacity and there are firm plans to expand generating capacity on Java and Bali alone by 4 GW over the next five years. However, demand growth continues to exceed the expansion of PLN capacity and privately owned capacity remains substantial (approximately 7.5 GW).

Electricity will remain a major priority of the government, which intends to continue expanding generating capacity and the distribution network substantially. At the end of the current

Sixth Five-Year Plan, PLN is expected to have some 22 GW of generating capacity in place. It still relies heavily on oil-fired plant with diesel sets representing about 20 per cent of capacity and fuel oil-fired plants about 45 per cent. Three-quarters of all the electricity generated by PLN in 1992 came from oil-fired plant. The bulk of the capacity owned by private generators is also diesel, generally operated inefficiently and at low load factors.

Measures are in hand to increase capacity based on non-oil sources, in particular coal, hydropower and geothermal. The first two units of the Suralaya coal-fired power station became operational in 1985 and a third unit is expected to start up shortly. These plants should then supply the bulk of electricity on Java enabling a number of fuel oil-fired plants to be taken out of commission. Two new coal-fired plants should be operating on Java by 1998 and others are planned for various islands.

The government plans to base most future generating needs on additional coal-fired plant and hydro, with nuclear remaining an open option. However, most of the growth in demand is on the densely populated island of Java and much of the coal on Sumatra and Kalimantan. To add to the problem, as mentioned earlier, almost all economic hydroelectric sites on Java have already been exploited.

Natural gas is an obvious, cheap and efficient substitute for oil in power generation. Curiously, there have been scarcely any new additions of gas-fired capacity in recent years. Indonesia has lagged behind other South East Asian countries in this respect although the situation is slowly being remedied. The government announced in September 1990 that it would actively encourage private investment in the generation of electricity. A number of power plant projects are currently being offered to private companies on a 'build, operate and transfer' basis and this route seems likely to encourage the greater use of gas. A pipeline from an Arco operated field off East Java is being built to serve a new gas-fired power station at Gresik near Surabaya. It seems likely that the other substantial gas reserves off Java and in Sumatra and elsewhere must eventually be tapped for power generation using private capital if the use of oil is to be restrained. In the longer term the development of an ASEAN electricity grid may help to bring about the use of the substantial energy resources of South East Asia in a balanced and cost effective way that could help to husband Indonesia's oil resources.

## Imbalances in the Supply and Demand of Petroleum Products

Energy policies must clearly continue to be directed towards moderating growth in domestic oil consumption if the country is to avoid becoming a net importer of oil within a few years. Apart from the substitution by other major forms of energy, steps have been taken to improve the efficiency with which oil products are used through introducing conservation laws and regulations and through promotional activities. There have also been a number of studies and surveys of the wide range of alternative energy sources that the country possesses. Although these studies have been of variable quality and perhaps excessive in number, they have resulted in some practical action.

Neither of these routes has, as yet, had a significant effect on domestic consumption of oil which has been growing at an average of just over 8 per cent per annum for the last five years. This is the chronic problem of the 'squeeze' between rapidly growing domestic needs for oil and a static or reducing availability which is discussed later in this chapter. There is also a problem of product imbalance, however, which the Indonesian government has, arguably, been equally unsuccessful in tackling. As Table 3.4 illustrates, demand for oil is heavily weighted towards middle distillates such as kerosene and gas oil and to a lesser extent to gasolines. This pattern of demand for oil products is common to many developing countries as urbanization and transportation grows and commercial fuels replace traditional fuels for cooking and lighting.

The government has been slow to change policies which have encouraged the use of kerosene and diesel through very substantial direct and indirect subsidies. It is this, together with increasing household prosperity, which has probably made the most significant contribution to distorting product demand. Other factors such as the chronic shortage of central electricity generating capacity, that has encouraged industry and others to generate their own electricity from diesel sets, have not helped.

**Table 3.4**: Domestic Sales of Petroleum Products

|  | 1987 | | 1993 | |
|---|---|---|---|---|
|  | *Million Barrels* | *Per Cent* | *Million Barrels* | *Per Cent* |
| Gasoline | 30.5 | 18 | 46.8 | 18 |
| Aviation Fuel | 4.3 | 3 | 9.3 | 3 |
| Kerosene | 43.4 | 26 | 54.5 | 20 |
| Gasoil | 54.1 | 33 | 105.1 | 40 |
| Diesel Fuel | 8.3 | 5 | 12.1 | 5 |
| Fuel Oil | 19.5 | 12 | 34.5 | 13 |
| Lubes | 1.8 | 1 | 3.0 | 1 |
| Others | 4.3 | 2 | - | - |
| Total | 166.2 | 100 | 265.3 | 100 |

Source: *Petroleum Report of Indonesia*, 1994

These elements are not unique to Indonesia and are now being tackled fairly vigorously; the politically bold step of removing direct fuel subsidies was taken in 1993. But new utility generating capacity has to compete for investment funds with many other key parts of the economy, as does the development of gas as a substitute for domestic use of gasoil and kerosene. With the economy still in the developing stage, the present concentration of oil demand growth on the middle distillates is likely to change only fairly slowly for some years to come.

On the refining side, capacity has usually been inadequate to match the pattern of demand and heavy reliance has had to be placed on refining outside the country and on product imports to match needs. The situation had been aggravated to some extent by the refining of heavy Indonesian crudes that produced a high proportion of heavy products such as fuel oil and waxy residues. Although out of balance in terms of product demand, gross crude refining capacity has for some years been in excess of domestic demand in overall terms although margins have been tight.

During the 1970s, there was a growing reliance on product imports from Singapore. This took place within the framework of a complex pattern of two-way trade in oil between the two countries, with the main feature of these arrangements being the processing of Indonesian crude in Singapore. By the early 1980s the spread of products manufactured had become seriously out of balance with the domestic market. Imports of kerosene and gasoil increased substantially whilst at the same time there were difficulties in finding markets for the waxy residue that remains after the initial treatment of Minas crude. To remedy this situation and to reduce dependence on foreign processors, a major programme for expanding and upgrading domestic refining was begun in 1983. By 1985, overall capacity was nearly 800,000 b/d with a 60,000 b/d hydrocracker installed at Balikpapan to produce kerosene and an 85,000 b/d hydrocracker at Dumai to process residual fuel to kerosene. The completion of these projects enabled Indonesia to substantially reduce refining in Singapore from 1987 onwards. This investment has gone some way to correcting the product imbalance although, as Table 3.5 shows, substantial imports are still necessary.

The overwhelming bulk of product exports consist of naphtha and low-sulphur waxy residue (LSWR).

Substantial growth in demand for gasolines and diesel fuel is likely to continue as the pace of motorization and urbanization puts increasing pressure on fuel for transport and household uses. Growth in demand for household kerosene will be lower over the coming years, partly because the Indonesian government has at last taken on the issue of subsidies but also because of the increasing availability and use of alternatives

**Table 3.5**: Product Imbalance 1993. Thousand Barrels Per Day

| | Production | Imports | Exports | Domestic Consumption | Stock Changes etc. |
|---|---|---|---|---|---|
| Gasoline | 171 | 5 | 30 | 128 | +18 |
| Kerosene | 146 | 27 | 2 | 174 | -3 |
| Diesel | 235 | 72 | - | 321 | -14 |
| Residual | 73 | 20 | - | 94 | -1 |
| Others[a] | 151 | - | 127 | 38 | -14 |
| Total | 776[b] | 124 | 159 | 755 | -14 |

Refinery Input:  810

a.  Includes Lubes and Petrochemicals
b.  Excludes Refinery Use and Loss

Source: *Petroleum Report of Indonesia*, 1994

such as LPG and natural gas as incomes rise. The reduction of subsidies on kerosene was particularly sensitive politically as it is an important home cooking fuel in lower-income households.

Even if all Pertamina's plans for new refineries do materialize, a small deficit of diesel fuel may well continue in the long term. There is still potential for limiting demand for diesel through changes in the fiscal and other treatment of diesel-powered vehicles. In practice the substitution of many diesel vehicles as well as diesel-powered generating sets will be difficult.

## Refining Policy

Indonesia currently has eight refineries with an installed capacity of some 868,000 b/d and an effective capacity said to be able to refine 905,000 b/d of crude oil. All the existing refineries are either on Sumatra or Java with the solitary exception of Balikpapan which is on Kalimantan.

Operating margins are not adequate and refineries are generally overloaded. Even with high throughputs, current capacity is unable to satisfy the present pattern of domestic demand for oil products. Overseas processing and the import of products has been rising during the 1990s so far and is expected to continue to do so. However, with new capacity due

**Table 3.6**: Refinery Capacity and Throughput in 1993. Thousand Barrels Per Calendar Day

|  | Effective Crude Distillation Capacity | Crude Processed |
|---|---|---|
| Balikpapan (E. Kalimantan) | 264 | 236 |
| Cilacap (C. Java) | 320 | 297 |
| Dumai (C. Sumatra) | 130 | 117 |
| Musi (S. Sumatra) | 136 | 113 |
| P. Brandon (N. Sumatra) | 5 | 5 |
| S. Pakning (C. Sumatra) | 45 | 39 |
| Wonokromo (E. Java) | 1 | - |
| Cepu (C. Java) | 4 | 3 |
| Total | 905 | 810 |

Sources: Economist Intelligence Unit, *Country Profile*, 1992; *Petroleum Report of Indonesia*, 1994; *International Petroleum Encyclopedia*; *Oil and Gas Journal*

onstream by the mid-1990s, there should then be a respite.

Almost all refining is carried out by Pertamina which owns and operates all the refineries shown in Table 3.6 except for Cepu, which may still be operated by Lemnigas. This makes Pertamina the sixteenth largest refiner in the world. The volumes of fuel used and 'lost' during the refining process were at one time relatively high, partly as a result of poor management, but now seem to be in line with normal refinery practice.

In line with the overall aim to reduce all product imports and replace crude exports by exports of products and petrochemicals, Pertamina has proposed a major expansion of capacity.[6] Much of it is designed for producing export products as a replacement for crude oil exports. Improvements and expansions are already in hand at several existing refineries and it had been hoped at one time that the new refineries would boost production by a very substantial 600,000 b/d by 1996. Investment in export refineries gives the opportunity for better margins than obtainable on the still restricted domestic market and adds value to the country's crude oil.

Commercial production from a new 125,000 b/d export oriented refinery (EXOR 1) at Balongan in West Java, began in November 1994. This refinery is a joint venture between Foster Wheeler, the Japanese consortium Japic and Mitsui. Financing involves a loan by the partners to Pertamina which is to be repaid through revenue from product sales.[7] The refinery benefits from UK government export credits and a BP offtake agreement negotiated when BP was still a UK government-owned company. Currently no oil products are piped to Jakarta from existing refineries even though the capital is the centre of demand on Java. A pipeline is now under construction from EXOR 1 to the Jakarta region so that although it is designated as an export refinery, in practice much of its production will be supplied to the domestic market.[8] The pipeline is being constructed on a build, own, operate and transfer basis and should help to alleviate pressure from increasing demand for gasoil and kerosene in and around Jakarta. The refinery is eventually expected to process 100,000 b/d of Duri crude and 25,000 b/d of Minas crude.

A second 120,000 b/d export refinery (EXOR 2) is planned at Sorong on Irian Jaya by Total, Unocal and Nichimen of

Japan. Part of the output would be for the domestic market, mainly middle distillates and aviation fuels, whilst other fuel would be for export to Japan and Korea. This refinery has been 'rescheduled' and its future is now somewhat uncertain.

Yet another 120,000 b/d refinery to be built at Tanjung Ubang on Bintan Island opposite Singapore (EXOR 3) has two-thirds of its potential output earmarked for export and would refine a mixture of Middle Eastern and Indonesian crudes. This refinery is to be financed by C. Itoh and BP who should be operating it independently from Pertamina. Another refinery is planned for Sungei Pakning to be built by Chevron and Mitsui near the existing one.

The fourth in the export refinery series (EXOR 4) with a capacity of 140,000 b/d has been approved for Dumai although the original planned date of completion has been rescheduled. It is planned to run this refinery on a mixture of Duri and Middle East crudes.

Debottlenecking and a residual conversion complex is also planned for the existing Cilacap refinery. The Musi refinery is due to be upgraded and possibly increased in capacity and Balikpapan modified to accommodate a wider range of heavy Indonesian and Middle East crudes. Pertamina is trying to raise the financing for Cilacap from Eximbank and Citicorp, with repayment through product exports from the refinery. These are likely to be mainly naphtha and low sulphur waxy residue as the middle distillates are needed for the domestic market.

There are also two domestic orientated refineries (PKDN 1 and 2) planned for Madura, East Java and for North Sumatra with a total capacity of 340,000 b/d.

This was an extremely ambitious and expensive programme with perhaps a hint of the old style grandiose schemes of Pertamina in the 1960s and 1970s. It was probably inevitable that late in 1991, as a result of the economy overheating and mounting foreign debt difficulties, a ceiling was put on commercial foreign debt which had the effect of postponing many planned refinery projects. The future of some of these projects is now highly uncertain. The government's committee to review foreign commercial borrowing rescheduled $10 billion of projects in the downstream sector. Included amongst them was the EXOR 4 refinery at Dumai which was shelved indefinitely, as was the residual catalytic cracking unit at Cilacap. The project for debottlenecking at Cilacap was, however, merely 'delayed'. The plans for Balongan (EXOR 1) and the upgrading of the Musi refinery went ahead. The proposal for the third export refinery on Bintan Island (EXOR 3) has yet to be reviewed.

This enforced postponement of the ambitious export refineries may turn out to be a blessing in disguise as the ability of the market to absorb all these export products seems rather uncertain. A survey of the current position on the refineries is shown in Table 3.7.

The original plans to boost production of refined products by 600,000 b/d would have put in place sufficient capacity to meet any likely domestic demand level and pattern to the end of the century. This capacity increase is now unlikely to be achieved and the retrenchment seems likely to result in a continuation of the tight product position. If domestic demand were to grow at, say, 3 per cent per annum to the year 2000, then existing capacity and that under construction may just be adequate. Growth at this low level seems unlikely unless there is a severe downturn in the economy or drastic price penalties on oil products leading to rapid substitution. If we were to

**Table 3.7**: Refinery Capacity Installed and Planned. Thousand Barrels Per Day

| | | |
|---|---|---|
| Existing Installed Refinery Capacity | 866 | |
| EXOR 1 (Export) Balongan | 125 | (Now onstream) |
| EXOR 2 (Export/Domestic) Sorong | 250 | (Shelved) |
| EXOR 3 (Export/Domestic) T. Ubang | 120 | (Approved, originally planned to be onstream in 1995 but under review) |
| EXOR 4 (Export) Dumai | 120 | (Approved, but shelved indefinitely) |
| PKDN 1 (Domestic) Madura | 140 | |
| PKDN 11 (Domestic) N. Sumatra | 200 | |
| Balikpapan Upgrading | 60 | (Approved) |
| Cilacap Expansion | 48 | (Approved) |
| Musi Expansion | - | |
| Total | 1,929 | |

Sources: *Petroleum Report of Indonesia*, 1994; *PIW, Energy Compass, Weekly Petroleum Argus*

assume growth at 6 to 8 per cent per annum, which is lower than recent experience, product demand would reach around 1.2 to 1.3 mb/d by the end of the century. Even if, in addition to existing refineries and those under construction, all planned capacity were in place by, say, the year 2000, then the 1.9 mb/d available would be just enough to meet domestic demand at this level and continue product exports at around current levels. However, there would be no scope to increase exports of products in place of crude oil which is the purpose of much of the capacity planned.

Some provisions do exist for foreign capital to be invested in refinery facilities. The government now allows full foreign equity in refinery projects that have a paid-up capital of at least $50 million or which are set up in areas outside Java. Under this investment policy, foreign investors have to reduce their equity share to 95 per cent within five years of the project coming onstream. After 20 years, equity is reduced to 49 per cent by divesting the balance to Indonesian nationals or companies. This policy seems to have had some success in attracting overseas interest in refinery investment although there are many uncertainties. However, there has recently been a setback because of the withdrawal of one of the major elements enabling foreign investors to secure bank loans. Formerly Pertamina gave a crude and product buy-back guarantee; generally they took back the middle distillates for the domestic market with the foreign investors exporting the naphtha and low sulphur waxy residue. The foreign currency proceeds are then used to pay off the loans. The withdrawal of guarantees under pressure from the IMF has necessitated renewed negotiations on the EXOR 3 project in particular and more tax incentives may have to be given.

A major disincentive to foreign investment in refineries is the firm control still retained by Pertamina on almost all marketing and distribution of products. Non-Indonesian oil companies have been effectively excluded from the downstream sector by the limited access to the market place and to some extent by the subsidized prices of oil products.

The market prospects for increased exports of products from the four planned export refineries may not, even if they do all go ahead, be very favourable. Over 85 per cent of current product exports are shipped to Japan which has an abundance of choice for high quality products from export refineries around the Pacific Rim. Japan is, however, likely to remain the main target for additional product sales although Pertamina is hoping, for example, to become a major supplier of reformulated gasoline to the west coast of the United States.

Indonesia seems committed to becoming a more prominent exporter of high quality light oil products in order to add value to its crude oil. This ambition will, apart from doubts about the market available, continue to be tempered by rising domestic demand and difficulties in maintaining a heavy refinery investment programme. There is a surfeit of refinery proposals in neighbouring countries of South East Asia and competition for foreign capital is fierce. It is foreign investors that Indonesia will have to rely heavily on if it is to maintain the refinery programme or at least revitalize some of the shelved projects. Apart from a change in attitude towards foreign investors taking a majority share of equity and having access to the domestic market, it must also be important to avoid further 'stop-go' policies.

## Liquefied Petroleum Gas

During the late 1980s, both the production and export of Liquefied Petroleum Gas (LPG) increased even more dramatically than that of Liquefied Natural Gas (LNG). In 1987 the country produced well under half a million tonnes of LPG. Production then accelerated in 1988 with the commencement of shipments to Japan under a long-term agreement. By 1990, 2.7 mt were being produced and this level has been maintained subsequently. The overwhelming bulk of LPG produced is exported, still mainly to Japan (see Table 3.8).

The long-term agreement with Japan signed in July 1986 calls for Indonesia to supply 1.95 mt (43,000 boe/d) of butane and propane each year to the end of the century. Under this agreement, the price of exports is determined annually on an f.o.b. basis linked to an average of the official prices posted by the main Gulf producers of LPG. Sales carry a premium of $3 per tonne in recognition of the advantage in shipping costs to Japan that Indonesia has over the Gulf.

In practice, sales under the agreement are well above the

**Table 3.8:** Production and Export of Liquefied Petroleum Gas. Thousand Tonnes

|                          | 1988  | 1989  | 1990  | 1991  | 1992  | 1993  |
|--------------------------|-------|-------|-------|-------|-------|-------|
| Production Ex. Refineries| 294   | 301   | 323   | 350   | 411   | 292   |
| Production Ex. Gas Plants| 959   | 2,271 | 2,416 | 2,388 | 2,373 | 2,484 |
| Total                    | 1,253 | 2,572 | 2,739 | 2,738 | 2,785 | 2,776 |
| Exports                  | 944   | 2,481 | 2,602 | 2,492 | 2,556 | 2,547 |

Source: *Petroleum Report of Indonesia*, 1994

level specified; for example, in 1993 2.4 mt were shipped to Japan, making Indonesia the second largest supplier of LPG to the Japanese market after Saudi Arabia. Some 95 per cent of current LPG exports are sales to Japan with the remainder going largely to Hong Kong, South Korea and Singapore.

The development of the gas fields at Arun and Bontang (Badak) has been the main stimulus behind the expansion of LPG exports. There are dedicated LPG processing plants at Arun and Badak, operated by Mobil and VICO, LPG plants at all four major refineries and several other field based plants operated by Arco, Union and Pertamina. There is also an LPG terminal at the port of Tanjung Uban owned and operated by Pertamina. An additional 400,000 tonne plant is planned for South Sumatra, although this is likely to have been affected by the recent retrenchment of major projects. Three-quarters of current production of around 2.7 million tonnes per annum is produced by the two facilities at Arun and Badak. Both were completed in 1988 with a notional capacity of 2.25 million tonnes per annum.

Exports of LPG make a useful contribution to the country's balance of payments with export earnings around $300–400 million per annum. There is substantial potential for additional LPG supplies from planned refinery expansion and particularly as an adjunct to new LNG units being built to increase sales of natural gas overseas.

The expanding markets of the Pacific Rim seem likely to continue to be the prime destination for additional supplies of Indonesian LPG. However, LPG could also be much more widely used by households and industry as an ideal substitute for kerosene at present. Domestic distribution facilities have been increasing slowly, although in 1993 only around 15 per cent of production was sold into the domestic market. Substantially greater use in the domestic market has been inhibited by the price disparity with kerosene and the lack of an adequate distribution network. However, the former has already been adjusted by the removal of subsidies on kerosene and there are signs of a more encouraging approach to the expansion of domestic use of LPG through the development of a widespread distribution network.

## Petrochemicals

Indonesia has long had ambitions to achieve a major domestic manufacturing capacity for chemicals as support for its expanding industrial sector. Falling oil prices led to the postponement of many large-scale public sector projects due to be constructed in the 1980s. However, the last few years have seen a revival of investment and the inauguration of numerous and wide-ranging chemical plants throughout the country. Tariff protection and low feedstock costs have been fundamental to much of the growth, and this has resulted in a substantial expansion from what was primarily a fertilizer oriented industry. Some 56 chemical plants are currently in operation, producing $4 billion worth of products of which 25 per cent are exported.

Despite this rather heady expansion, compared with other major oil and gas producers as well as other countries in the region, Indonesia still lags in the development of production facilities for many basic petrochemicals.

Fertilizer production was a national priority in the 1960s and 1970s to assure self-sufficiency in rice production. This programme was a major success with considerable help from international aid agencies and artificially low feedstock prices. The Urea industry was expanded substantially and, as a result, since the late 1970s Indonesia has been an exporter of fertilizer. There are now five plants throughout the country producing 5 mt of nitrogenous fertilizers from natural gas feedstocks.

The consumption of chemicals is forecast to continue to grow rapidly as the manufacturing base expands. For example, the demand for ethylene, methanol and polypropylene is expected

**Table 3.9:**   Installed Capacity of Selected Petrochemicals. 1991/1992.
Thousand Tonnes

| | |
|---|---|
| Adhesive Resin | 1,033 |
| Ammonia | 3,248 |
| Benzene | 123 |
| Polypropylene | 370 |
| PTA | 150 |
| PVC | 164 |
| Methanol | 330 |
| Urea | 4,940 |
| Paraxlene | 270 |
| Nylon Tyre Cord | 28 |
| Carbon Black | 90 |

Source: *Petroleum Report of Indonesia,* 1993

to almost double by the end of the 1990s. This was recognized in the Fifth Five-Year Development Plan (1989 to 1994) which gave priority to the further development of basic petrochemical industries, particularly olefins and aromatics.

In 1988, a major new expansion programme for the chemical industry was put in motion involving public and private sector investments of more than $4.5 billion. There were 21 separate projects which were all due to become operational in the first half of the 1990s. They included some 1.8 mt of additional methanol capacity. As with the refinery projects, a number of these projects have had to be rescheduled and their present status is uncertain.

As for refineries, the 1992 foreign investment regulations permitting 100 per cent foreign ownership of projects valued in excess of $50 million will help the industry. This, with an increasingly flexible approach to the structure of investment and ownership, may help to get a number of stalled plants underway. These include the $2 billion Chandri Asri olefins complex at Cilegon in West Java, to produce ethylene, propylene and additional downstream products, and a major $1.3 billion aromatics plant at Arun, North Sumatra. Both were rescheduled in 1991 but interest is continuing and some of the early stages of construction have been completed. The olefins project appears to be going ahead amid some controversy.[9] The two refineries planned for Riau in West Sumatra are part of plans to develop a petrochemical industry on the island.

In the past, the major chemical plants that have been built or proposed have sometimes been based more on considerations of 'prestige' than of sound practicality and commercialism. If Indonesia is to have the chemicals industry appropriate to a major industrial country it needs to continue to build up its capabilities at least at the pace originally planned. The old attitudes towards chemical plants as a source of all sorts of unofficial financial and other benefits is changing but will need to change further if scarce capital is to be attracted and utilized efficiently. With its substantial natural gas resources particularly suitable as chemical feedstocks, Indonesia has the ability to become a major petrochemical producer and player in Asian chemical markets.

## The Outlook for Oil: Can the 'Oil Squeeze' be Avoided?

Domestic demand for oil products has shown little sign of slowing down in the 1990s. Indeed in 1992, total sales grew at 8.4 per cent compared with 7.5 per cent the year before. Government enforced increases in fuel prices in August 1991 helped to keep growth in check but the changes in January 1993, when most product prices were increased by more than 20 per cent, slowed growth during the year. Even with these moves to more realistic pricing and a certain amount of price elasticity, however, domestic demand for oil seems likely to continue to grow well into the next century at least. Substitution by gas and coal and efficiency improvements will help to restrain growth, although the inexorable growth of population, urbanization and mobility seems likely to ensure that growth will be substantial.

One view expressed in a World Bank publication by Imran and Barnes is that the share of oil in primary energy demand could fall to 44 per cent by 2010, with substantial increases in the contribution of coal and gas.[10] This projection represents an optimistic view of the progress of substitution and efficiency savings and would result in an increase in domestic oil demand of just 200,000 b/d by the year 2010. This is very modest given that in the ten years between 1982 and 1992, for example, domestic demand for oil increased by 265,000 b/d.

**Table 3.10:**   Shares in Commercial Primary Energy Demand. Per Cent

|                  | 1990 | 2000 | 2010 |
|------------------|------|------|------|
| Oil              | 62   | 54   | 44   |
| Coal             | 3    | 14   | 19   |
| Natural Gas      | 27   | 25   | 30   |
| Hydropower etc.  | 7    | 7    | 7    |
| Total            | 100  | 100  | 100  |

Source: M. Imran & P. Barnes, *Energy Demand in Developing Countries*, 1990

**Table 3.11:**   Projected Demand for Primary Commercial Energy. Million Barrels of Oil Equivalent Per Day

|                  | 1992 | 2010 |
|------------------|------|------|
| Oil              | 0.7  | 1.6  |
| Natural Gas      | 0.4  | 0.7  |
| Coal             | 0.1  | 0.3  |
| Hydropower etc.  | 0.1  | 0.2  |
| Total            | 1.3  | 2.8  |

Source: OIES forecasts

The actual demand for additional oil in the domestic market, spurred on by the liberalization of the economy, may well turn out to be considerably in excess of these projections. Certainly, without very substantial investment in domestic gas use combined with much greater use of coal for electricity generation than currently seems likely, we would not expect the proportion of oil in total commercial energy demand to fall below 55 per cent or so.

On the basis of GNP increasing at an average annual rate of around 6 per cent, as during the past few years, we would expect commercial primary energy demand to reach around 2.8 mboe/d by 2010. This compares with 1.3 mboe/d in 1992. Even with substantial expansion in domestic gas use and additional coal and hydro use for power generation, it is unlikely that the demand for oil will be below 1.5 to 1.6 mb/d by 2010.[11]

**Table 3.12:** Oil Demand by Markets. Million Barrels of Oil Equivalent Per Day

| | 1992 | 2010 | Annual Average Increase Per Cent |
|---|---|---|---|
| Transport | 0.26 | 0.76 | 6.2 |
| Industry | 0.14 | 0.24 | 3.1 |
| Residential+Services | 0.16 | 0.26 | 2.8 |
| Electricity Generation | 0.10 | 0.12 | 1.1 |
| Others | 0.08 | 0.21 | 5.6 |
| Total | 0.74 | 1.59 | 4.4 |

Source: Author's forecasts

Although demand for oil will continue to increase significantly in the industrial and residential markets and for electricity generation in the early part of the period, the fastest growing use will be for transport – which is likely to remain the largest single user of oil products. It is this market, in which liquid fuels are largely unsubstitutable, that will need to be restrained through improved efficiency and other measures if oil use is not to more than double by the year 2010, or earlier (see Appendix 10 for more detailed projections).

A cheap oil policy combined with a relatively high rate of economic growth, has led in the past to rapid growth in the domestic consumption of oil. There is a real threat that oil demand could outstrip oil production in just a few years if such growth rates continue. In recent years, consumption has grown at an average annual increase of around 8 per cent. Growth may already have slackened somewhat in 1994 and 1995. It is hoped that efficiency measures and further substitution by natural gas, coal and electricity encouraged by the recent price rises, will be able to keep demand growth rates below those of recent years.

As Figure 3.1 shows, if growth in domestic demand could be kept down to about 4.5 per cent annual average increase and crude oil production increased slightly to peak at around 1.9 mb/d in the late 1990s, net oil available for export could be maintained close to its current level for a few years. By the year 2010 however, even with demand growth at this relatively low

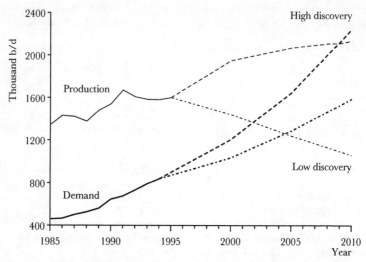

Sources:  *BP Statistical Review of World Energy*; *Twentieth Century Petroleum Statistics*;
author's own projections

**Figure 3.1** The Export Squeeze

rate in comparison with the past, no oil at all would be available
for export on a net basis.

It is only if production can be increased to well over 2 mb/d
that exports could be maintained at current levels against any
reasonable view of future domestic demand for oil. Figure 3.1
underlines the necessity of increasing and sustaining oil
production levels as well as moderating domestic oil demand in
order to achieve broad economic prosperity and to avoid
political disaster. Pertamina has been projecting that annual
growth in fuel consumption will continue at 6.5 per cent through
to the end of the century. This would rapidly reduce the
country's surplus of crude oil for export unless production could
be raised and substitution increased.

It will not be enough just to maintain current levels of
production and to restrain domestic demand for oil. Unless
further major capital expenditures are actually made in
expanding and upgrading refining capacity, the country will
continue to rely on imports of refined products and crude oil.
As well as providing a replacement for falling export revenues

from oil, the faster development of Indonesia's substantial gas resources is one of the major keys to reducing the domestic consumption of oil.

## Notes

1. For example, waste wood and vegetable matter may have an efficiency in thermal terms of perhaps 10 per cent when used for cooking. Kerosene used in simple burners may have an efficiency of 40 per cent and LPG perhaps 45 per cent or more. US Dept. of Commerce. 'Energy Inter-relationships' 6/77.
2. Not taking into account gas losses and use in LNG plants. The shares of oil and gas in energy demand can vary considerably for the same period. Much depends on the definition of domestic consumption. Including the gas plant use (the 'losses' between net production and actual output from the LNG plants in domestic consumption) as in the energy matrix reduces oil's share to just under 60 per cent in 1992 and increases gas to 30 per cent.
3. 6.7 per cent average annual increase between 1982 and 1992 but 8.4 per cent annual average increase over the five years 1987 to 1992. *BP Statistical Review of World Energy*, 1993.
4. M. Imran and P. Barnes, *Energy Demand in the Developing Countries*, World Bank, 1990.
5. Growth in energy demand (per cent average annual increase) between 1987 and 1992. Electricity generation, 11.6; Transport, 8.8; Industry, 9.6; Domestic, 4.2. Growth in demand for oil products over a similar period; Mogas and automotive diesel, 10.3 per cent; Fuel oil for power generation, 9.8 per cent; Kerosene 2.2 per cent. *Petroleum Report of Indonesia*.
6. This was part of an ambitious master plan formulated by Pertamina in the late 1980s which also included the construction of several large petrochemical complexes, the addition of a new LNG train to the existing one at Bontang and a number of major oil and gas projects. The total cost of the 18 or so projects was estimated at nearly $30 billion in 1991 dollars. As a result of Presidential Decree 39 issued late in 1991, a number of these projects were either deferred or cancelled. A committee to review foreign currency borrowing was established at the same time, and this ensured that Pertamina revised its master plan to the present, less ambitious scale. Thus, any likelihood of Pertamina going down the disastrous lavish spending road of the 1970s was prevented.
7. Financing is partly from UK government export credits and a BP offtake agreement. *Petroleum Report of Indonesia*.
8. Most gasoline used in Indonesia contains lead and the new EXOR 1 refinery will produce some High Octane Mogas Components for consumption in the Jakarta region. Much of the country's plan for producing more environmentally friendly oil products was stopped when Pertamin's master plan was halted.

9. This may be a prime example of economic nationalism at work. Bimantara is a huge contractor and there is pressure to keep such a substantial and rewarding project alive. The 'technocrats' fear that once the olefins plant is completed, import bans will be put in place so that local producers of plastics will not be able to get their raw materials from the cheapest sources. *The Economist,* 17 April, 1993.

10. Oil demand was projected to reach 705,000 boe/d in the year 2000 and 836,000 boe/d in the year 2010 in the context of a 'high growth and generally economically successful environment'.

11. There are, of course, other views. A projection by the East–West Centre quoted in the *Oil and Gas Journal* of 11 April, 1994 puts domestic demand for oil at 802,000 b/d in 1995 but apparently only at 804,000 b/d in 2000.

# 4   NATURAL GAS:
# THE BASIS FOR FUTURE PROSPERITY

## Introduction

From producing barely 1 billion cubic metres (bcm) per annum
of natural gas in the early 1970s, all of which was used locally,
Indonesia has become the world's leading exporter of liquefied
natural gas, supplying nearly 40 per cent of world trade. The
gross revenues from sales of LNG exceeded $4 billion in both
1991 and 1992 and represented 14 per cent of the country's
export earnings. 35 per cent of export earnings generated from
hydrocarbons now come from gas compared with only 15 per
cent in 1980. On a net basis, after taking into account the cost
of crude and oil product imports, LNG is now roughly comparable to oil as a generator of foreign exchange and contributor
to the balance of payments.

The resource base for gas seems substantial and, given the
right investment conditions, natural gas should become increasingly important to the economy of Indonesia. Indeed, revenues
from gas exports could well exceed those from oil within a year
or two. The growth in importance of gas to the economy will
be not only in the form of additional exports but increasingly
from its role as a substitute for oil in the domestic market. The
policy decisions to be made on the direction and pace of future
gas development are fundamental to the economic prosperity
of the country.

## The Resource Base

It is only comparatively recently that contractors have actively
explored for gas. In the past, pricing conditions for gas and the
lack of markets did not favour the development or proving up
of reserves. The major accumulations of gas discovered in the
early 1970s were initially considered to be of limited use. The
laborious process of developing the markets for this gas in the
form of LNG exports had to be completed first. The rise in oil
prices in the 1970s, the success of the new export market and
the realization that oil reserves were not keeping pace with
demand, increased interest in the country's gas potential.

Currently, Indonesia has some 30 per cent of all gas reserves in South East Asia and Australasia. Deposits occur in tertiary limestone and clastic reservoirs and gas is produced from associated and non-associated deposits both on and offshore. The bulk of reserves are, however, of non-associated gas. Total proven reserves of natural gas in Indonesia are said to have been around 1,800 bcm or 64 trillion standard cubic feet (scf) at the end of 1992.[1] Such a volume represents some 34 years of production at current rates. This is at least two or three times the reserves/production ratio for oil, depending on which reserves estimates are used in comparison. Potential gas reserves represent at least another 1,000 bcm or 37 trillion cubic feet (tcf). Proven reserves seem likely to increase substantially, partly because of new discoveries but also through the upgrading of known 'technical' reserves. Their classification into the proven category depends on the opening up of new export and domestic markets to make them 'economic'. Thus, the more markets are available the more proven reserves could increase to meet them.

Reserves are widely distributed, with major accumulations in northern Sumatra and eastern Kalimantan and others off Java and elsewhere (see Table 4.1). Some 40 per cent of reserves are in the Belida field in the area off Natuna Island.[2]

The overall gas resource base is sometimes put at between two to four times the reserve estimate. Pertamina is bullish about the potential from the frontier areas, apparently believing that they contain an additional 219 bcf of gas, of which 172 are

**Table 4.1**:  Distribution of Gas Reserves. 1993.  Per Cent

| | |
|---|---|
| Natuna | 41 |
| N. Sumatra | 16 |
| C. Sumatra | 5 |
| S. Sumatra | 1 |
| W. Java | 7 |
| E. Java | 3 |
| E. Kalimantan | 25 |
| Sulawesi | 1 |
| Irian Jaya | 1 |
| Total | 100 |

Source: *Petroleum Report of Indonesia*, 1994

offshore.[3] There is great uncertainty about all these estimates and numbers do not in themselves mean a great deal. It does seem likely, however, that there are very substantial volumes of gas yet to be discovered. Both reserve and resource estimates will be significantly enhanced with further exploration and development, particularly now that additional gas reserves are seen as an exploration target on their own with a ready and valuable market in an increasing number of locations. Whatever the validity of individual estimates it is clear that natural gas is no longer a mere by-product of oil exploration.

## Present Production, Structure and Contractual Conditions

The Dutch colonial government built some towns gas systems but these were based solely on coal conversion. It is only since the early 1970s that Indonesia has invested in the infrastructure needed to produce, transport and utilize natural gas. Net annual gas production has grown from 1.2 bcm in 1970 to nearly 56 bcm (1980 bcf) at present. Around 70 per cent of the gas is liquefied as LNG for export; the remainder is used for LPG production or direct consumption in the domestic market (see Table 4.2).

The gas industry is at present largely based on two major gas and condensate fields, at Arun in northern Sumatra and at Badak (Bontang port) in East Kalimantan. These were both discovered in the early 1970s by Mobil Oil and Huffco respectively. They were eventually brought into production in 1977 and 1978, with the establishment of a liquefaction industry. Reserves in

**Table 4.2:**  Natural Gas Production and Use. Billion Standard Cubic Feet

|      | *Gross Production* | *Own Use* | *Flared* | *Marketed* |
|------|--------------------|-----------|----------|------------|
| 1980 | 1,046              | 198       | 242      | 606        |
| 1985 | 1,580              | 377       | 129      | 1,074      |
| 1990 | 2,159              | 454       | 167      | 1,538      |
| 1991 | 2,462              | 416       | 203      | 1,743      |
| 1992 | 2,583              | 525       | 217      | 1,840      |
| 1993 | 2,662              | 541       | 211      | 1,910      |

Source: *Petroleum Report of Indonesia*, 1994

these fields are estimated to be at least 11.9 trillion scf for Arun and 5.4 trillion scf for Badak.

As with oil, Pertamina has the sole rights to exploration and development in the gas industry. In practice, under 10 per cent of total gas was actually produced by Pertamina in 1993. As Table 4.3 shows, Mobil and Vico between them produced 67 per cent of Indonesia's gas. Many of the other producers are rather small players in the oil and gas business both internationally and in Indonesia. However, a number of companies, particularly Total, have been increasing in significance in recent years.

The Second 25-Year Development Plan envisages that gas production will rise to 3,300 billion scf by the last year of the Plan, 2019. In the light of the potential resources and the growing emphasis on gas markets in Indonesia and the rest of South East Asia, this appears rather conservative. Much hinges on the way in which LNG trade in the region develops and on the terms offered by the Indonesian government to its contractors.

The terms of production-sharing contracts under which foreign companies produce natural gas are broadly similar to

**Table 4.3:**   Natural Gas Production in 1993

|  | Billion Standard Cubic Feet | Per Cent |
|---|---|---|
| Pertamina | 255 | 9.6 |
| Stanvac | 30 | 1.1 |
| Arco | 94 | 3.5 |
| Asamera | 48 | 1.8 |
| Vico (Huffco) | 546 | 20.5 |
| Inpex | 152 | 5.7 |
| Mobil | 1,207 | 45.3 |
| Total | 116 | 4.4 |
| Union | 63 | 2.4 |
| Caltex | 35 | 1.3 |
| Marathon | 22 | 0.8 |
| Maxus | 19 | 0.7 |
| Other | 75 | 2.9 |
| Total | 2,662 | 100.0 |

Source: *Indonesia: Source Book*

those for oil. There are some differences in the terms in recognition of the higher up-front costs involved in developing gas. Capital investment can be fully recovered and, from the early days of the contracts, there has been no ceiling on the ratio of cost recovery to total production. The production-sharing ratio in the original contracts was on a basis of 70 per cent to the government and 30 per cent to the contractor when it was 85/15 per cent under the oil contracts. In the incentives package of 31 August, 1992, the equity split in gas contracts was made even more favourable in new contract areas in both conventional and frontier areas. The government share of gas produced in deepwater, for example, was reduced to 55 per cent.[4]

Gas pricing has not always been orientated adequately towards field economics in the past, especially for gas used in the domestic market. It is the government's intention that it should now be more related to the economic returns of new projects.[5] Whether this professed change of attitude and the current terms for new contracts will be enough to encourage more rapid development is yet to be seen.

### Trade in Liquefied Natural Gas (LNG)

Although not the first country to export liquefied gas on a regular basis, it can be said that Indonesia virtually created the world LNG market in the 1970s. Today it remains the leading LNG exporter with nearly 40 per cent of world trade. LNG exports are now the country's largest single earner of foreign exchange.

At present, there are 12 liquefaction trains, six at Arun in North Sumatra and six at Bontang on the Badak field in East Kalimantan. A total notional capacity of 22 mt is in place at present with an additional train of 2.3 mt well advanced in the planning stage for Bontang. Table 4.4 provides further details. The stated capacities are regularly exceeded.

All existing LNG capacity is fully contracted at present. Indeed, actual sales during the 1990s have been well in excess of the originally contracted tonnages and of rated plant capacity. This over-production in relation to design capacity is fairly normal with LNG plants and the Indonesian plants have all been designed with relatively large operating margins.

**Table 4.4**:  LNG Production Capacity

|  | Start Up Date | Number of Trains | Design Capacity Million Tonnes Per Annum |
|---|---|---|---|
| *Badak (Bontang)* | | | |
| A/B | 8/77 | 2 | 4.3 |
| C/D | 10/83 | 2 | 4.3 |
| E | 12/89 | 1 | 2.3 |
| F | 11/93 | 1 | 2.3 |
| G | 1998 | 1 | 2.3 |
| H (Originally Planned for 1996) | | | |
| | | | |
| *Arun* | | | |
| A/B/C | 10/78 | 3 | 4.5 |
| D/E | 3/84 | 2 | 3.0 |
| F | 10/86 | 1 | 1.5 |
| G (Planned for 1997 But Now Later) | | 1 | 2.0 |
| | | | |
| Total Capacity in Place in 1994 | | | 22.2 |
| (Actual Sales in 1993: 23.7) | | | |

Trains A to D at Bontang are currently undergoing debottlenecking for completion during 1994

Sources: *Petroleum Report of Indonesia, Gas Matters*

Production levels of 140 per cent of capacity at Bontang and 120 per cent at Arun have been regularly achieved! This has enabled Pertamina to sell LNG in excess of their long-term contractual obligations.

Sales in 1992 reached 23.4 mt per annum (1,120 billion Btu), of which 80 per cent went to Japan, 14 per cent to South Korea and the balance to Taiwan. In 1993, sales increased slightly to 23.7 mt, of which 77 per cent went to Japan and 16 per cent to South Korea. According to Minister Sudjana it is hoped to export some 26 mt in the financial year 1994/95 with sales of around 28 mt planned for the year 1998/99. This is a fairly modest and sensible ambition which hinges on the completion of the new train at Badak. Of total sales in 1992, the overwhelming bulk, 21.8 mt, were sold under long-term contracts. Details of the contracts currently in force or about to be applied are shown in Table 4.5.

**Table 4.5**: Existing Gas Contracts in Operation

| Destination | First Delivery | Duration (Years) | Million Tonnes Per Annum | Original Price Base | Source |
|---|---|---|---|---|---|
| Japan (1) | 1977 | 23 | 3.2 | (A) | Badak |
| Japan (1) | 1978 | 23 | 4.3 | (A) | Arun |
| Japan (2) | 1983 | 20 | 3.2 | (B) | Badak |
| Japan (2) | 1983 | 17 | 0.7 | (E) | Badak/Arun |
| Japan (3) | 1984 | 20 | 3.3 | (B) | Arun |
| Korea (4) | 1986 | 20 | 2.0 | c.i.f. | Arun |
| Japan (5) | 1987 | 7 | 0.7 | c.i.f. | Badak/Arun |
| Japan (6) | 1988 | 5.5 | 0.4 | (C) | Badak/Arun |
| Japan (6) | 1988 | 9.5 | 0.1 | (C) | Badak/Arun |
| Taiwan (7) | 1990 | 20 | 1.5-1.9 | n.a. | Badak |
| Japan (11) | 1990 | 15 | 0.5 | n.a. | |
| Japan (10) | 1990 | 3 | 0.2 | n.a. | |
| Korea (4) | 1992 | 15 | 0.3 | (F) | Badak |
| Korea (4) | 1992 | 3 | 0.9 | n.a. | Arun |
| | | | | | |
| Total to Japan | | 16.6 | (Sales in 1993: 18.6) | | |
| Total to Korea | | 3.2 | (Sales in 1993: 3.4) | | |
| Total to Taiwan | | 1.5-1.9 | (Sales in 1993: 1.7) | | |
| Grand Total | | 20.7-21.1 | (Sales in 1993: 23.7) | | |

*Other Gas Contracts*

| Destination | First Delivery | Duration | Million Tonnes | Original Price Base | Source |
|---|---|---|---|---|---|
| Japan (8) | 1994 | 20 | 2.0-2.3 | (D) | Badak |
| Korea (4) | 1994 | 20 | 2.0 | f.o.b. | Badak |
| Japan (9) | 1996 | 21 | 0.2-0.4 | n.a. | Badak |
| Taiwan (7) | 1998 | 17 | 1.9 | n.a. | Badak |
| Korea (4) | 1998 | 19 | 1.0 | f.o.b./c.i.f. | Badak |

Notes: (A) 1973 Agreement   (B) 1981 Agreement
(C) 'Super Deal'   (D) 1973 Agreement with Small Discount
(E) Additional Contracts Based on 1973 Agreement
(F) Expansion of Earlier c.i.f. Contract

Importer/Buyer: (1) Importer: Nissho Iwai for Chubu Electric, Kansai Electric, Kyusha Electric, Osaka Gas and Nippon Steel. (2) Importer: Nissho Iwai for Chubu Electric, Kansai Electric, Kyusha Electric, Osaka Gas, Tokyo Electric, Tohoku Electric and Toho Gas (3) Importer: Mitsubishi for Tohoku Electric and Tokyo Electric   (4) Korea Gas (5) Importer: Nissho Iwai for Chubu Electric et al (6) Osaka Gas, Toho Gas (7) China Petroleum Co.   (8) Tokyo Gas, Osaka Gas, Toho Gas (9) Nihon Gas, Hiroshima Gas (10) Kansai Electric (11) Tohoku Electric, Tokyo Gas

Sources: *Cedigaz News Report*; *Gas Matters*; *Energy Policy*; *BP Gas Review*; *FT International Gas Report*

As with most international LNG schemes, long-term main contracts cover the bulk of sales to Japan and it is these two original contracts of 1973 and 1981 that have set the tone and conditions for all the subsequent sales. The first contracts signed in 1973, provided initially for deliveries from 1977 to the year 2000 of a total tonnage of 7.5 mt per annum, 4.3 from Arun and 3.2 from Badak. The other set of contracts, signed in 1981, originally provided for the delivery of 6.5 mt per annum for 20 years from 1984 to 2004.

Although these contracts are set to run to the end of the century and beyond, serious negotiations were already underway in 1994 with a view to their extension. The availability of gas to support the extension of these contracts and the further expansion of gas exports which the country needs, is one of the most crucial elements in the future of the Indonesian economy.[6] The main contractual conditions under which LNG is exported are covered in the next section.

## Contractual Terms for Gas Sales

S. Padmosukismo, the head of the Energy Ministry's oil and gas section (Migas), has described three generations of gas pricing policy in Indonesia.[7] The first was designed to stop gas being flared in excessive quantities. A fixed 65c per mBtu was offered to encourage gas use for fertilizer manufacture. This was, and is, a common initial route for many developing countries. An otherwise waste product is used and at the same time a national fertilizer industry on which to build self-sufficiency in basic foods is encouraged. The next era was basically one of export pricing involving the sale of LNG to foreign buyers with the price linked to that of crude oil. The third and most recent era is one where prices are designed to encourage the development of fields for broader domestic use. This involves fixed prices related to the development costs of the specific field involved. The two recent major developments for domestic use, Arco's Offshore N.W. Java Gas Project and the Pagerungan field were both developed on this basis. The introduction of some form of indexing and setting prices in line with the 'economic value' of the gas rather than fixed, cost based, prices is likely to be one key to faster development of gas for domestic use.

At present, however, the bulk of gas is exported and LNG exports will remain of paramount importance to the economy. The way in which the terms in the LNG contracts have developed and are allowed to develop in future are thus of considerable significance. There are two base load prices for the LNG contracts; one applicable to the first, 1973, c.i.f. contracts now covering 8.3 mt and the other higher price applicable to the 1981 f.o.b. contracts to supply 6.5 mt.

The original 1973 contract called for c.i.f. LNG prices to be 90 per cent linked on a thermal equivalent basis to the average selling price of a basket of 20 Indonesian crudes. The 10 per cent is an inflating element. This contract was reportedly the first in the Asian Pacific LNG trade to include a take-or-pay condition. The only information available on the extent of such obligations is an indicated range of 3–10 per cent of annual contract volumes. In addition, the contract contains a floor price, a currency adjustment clause and a minimum Btu content per delivery and per year. The sellers are obliged to first offer all volumes produced in excess of contract volumes to the original contract buyers. Most of the investment capital required for the facilities at Badak and Arun to meet this contract, approximately 85 per cent of the total, came from Japanese sources – the financing being largely channelled through Jilco.

The 1981 contract has a pricing formula involving f.o.b. prices and a 100 per cent linkage with Indonesian crudes. Funds for this venture were also provided by Japanese buyers through prepayment for the LNG volumes to be delivered over ten years. The LNG vessels used under the f.o.b. contracts are Japanese owned and operated whilst those under the c.i.f. contracts are under charter to Pertamina. The actual netbacks vary widely but are believed to compare very favourably with LNG projects outside Indonesia, largely because of the employment of some vessels built in the 1970s.

Both Bontang and Arun have been operating in excess of their design capacities for some years and excess tonnages have been offered to the buyers under the terms of the 1973 contract. However, it was not until 1983 that contracts were actually signed for additional tonnages to be delivered to the original 1973 buyers. These covered the delivery of an additional 0.6 to 0.8 mt per annum until the expiry of the original 1973 contract in 2000.

Some other LNG production in excess of that available for the main long-term contracts is sold on a short-term basis. Certain 'super deal' contracts with Osaka gas and Toho gas are of limited duration. In practice, the arrangements for these cargoes are fairly flexible and enable extra cargoes to be delivered when available.

In the past, prices for short-term sales have involved some discounting, particularly on the transport element. As a result of changing market conditions, their prices are now reported to be in line with the basis laid down in the 1973 contract. Although that formula gives a slightly lower return than the 1981 contract formula, this route seems to be favoured by the Indonesian government as more acceptable for long-term market retention.

After the oil price collapse of 1986 and the abandonment of the Government Selling Price (GSP) as a pricing mechanism for crude oil exports, Indonesia's refusal to break the link with GSP for gas drew sharp criticism from Japanese customers. Eventually, after prolonged negotiations, Indonesia agreed in September 1986 to refund $577 million over a period of five years. Nonetheless, the issue remained a source of friction for some time and led to the announcement in February 1989 that prices would be lowered through linkage to actual selling prices. Price differentials between the 1973 contracts and the higher 1981 contracts were reduced by 8c per mBtu in 1989 and 1990. However shipping costs differ, making the 1981 price an estimated 0.3–0.4c per mBtu higher delivered in Japan.

The c.i.f. price for deliveries in 1991 averaged over all shipments to Japan under both long- and short-term contracts was $3.85 per mBtu. Prices generally have fallen under the contractual terms in 1992; the average in 1992 was $3.70 per mBtu.[8] By October 1993, the price had fallen to 3.36 per mBtu and the average over 1993 was $3.55, some 4 per cent lower than 1992.

The original contracts for deliveries of gas to Korea called for indexation to the official prices for Indonesian crudes imported by Korea. Presumably this has now been changed to linkage with actual selling prices. The contract with Taiwan is believed to be 90 per cent linked with Indonesian crude export prices with the remaining 10 per cent following a freight formula. There is also believed to be a take-or-pay formula applicable to at least 64 per cent of the annual contract tonnages. In addition, the contract gives options to add extra shipments to the contracted tonnages. The average price for deliveries to Korea in 1993 was $3.36 per mBtu ($3.65 in 1992).

The Indonesian government does seem to be sensitive to the market and, albeit with reluctance, has in the past been prepared to show flexibility. Certainly, its contractual policy, seen in terms of sales in relation to capacity and the netback achieved, appears to have been successful.

Indonesian gas is well placed geographically, which will continue to give it competitive freight costs to meet growth in gas demand in Japan and elsewhere in South East Asia. As a very experienced supplier, with ongoing long-term contracts, sound commercial relationships and established plant near to being fully depreciated, Pertamina appears to be in a relatively strong position at the moment. There is, however, considerable competition developing from other existing or potential suppliers in Australia, Malaysia, Alaska, Sakhalin Island and elsewhere to serve the Asian market. The extent of the long-term potential of this market is not clear and various 'authoritative' estimates are bandied around for commercial reasons. The real potential for additional sales and the share that Indonesia could supply into the next century is very uncertain. There are also uncertainties concerning the future availability of gas supplies in Indonesia and the government's willingness to provide the necessary incentives to attract the investment and expertise that will bring the gas to market.

## The Domestic Market

As well as being liquefied for export, natural gas is used in the domestic market. At present this is largely as a feedstock for fertilizer plants. It is also used to produce methanol, in refineries, by a handful of industrial users such as the Krakatau steel plant and as towns gas in a few urban centres. There is already a local pipeline system around Jakarta fed from Arco's nearby offshore fields. Small volumes of gas are also used in compressed form (CNG) in Jakarta, mainly for taxis. Nonetheless, as Table 4.6 shows, domestic use is still very modest compared with gas exports.

**Table 4.6:** Natural Gas Use in 1993. Per Cent of Gross Production

| | |
|---|---|
| Industry Own Use | 20 |
| Flared | 8 |
| State Electricity | 1 |
| City Gas | 1 |
| Fertilizer Plants | 8 |
| Cement Plants | Negligible |
| Refineries | 1 |
| LPG/Lex Plants | 2 |
| LNG Plants | 57 |
| Others | 2 |
| | 100   (2,663 bcf or 75 bcm) |

Source: *Petroleum Report of Indonesia*, 1994

In the past, priority was given to developing gas for export. The development of the Arco Pagerungan field in East Java at the beginning of 1991 was the first time that a major gas field in Indonesia had been developed solely for the domestic market. The need to meet growing energy needs and to substitute for oil, particularly on Java, has shifted emphasis and led to a flurry of new gas projects for domestic consumption. During 1991 there was an examination of the domestic sector by the government and the World Bank to formulate a development strategy for the greater use of gas. This is now the basic document for gas strategy and includes the following conclusions:

- The use of non-exportable gas in power generation and industry is desirable because of economic benefits (i.e. net-back values) that are higher than the economic cost of the oil;
- Projected consumption of gas is sufficiently large to invest in gas transmission infrastructure;
- Pricing and institutional changes are necessary to provide incentives to the production sharing contractors to develop proven and potential reserves and to embark on new exploration.

The Pertamina Senior Vice President Baharuddin, stated early in 1992 that Indonesia could easily absorb much of its own gas and stressed that local priorities can no longer be ignored. This may partly have been a commercial negotiating message aimed at potential LNG buyers. Nonetheless, increasingly expensive additions to LNG capacity must be considered in the light of cheaper, if less financially rewarding, domestic pipeline alternatives. However, the economics of using gas internally must be improving considerably through the growing use of efficient combined-cycle gas-fired power plants.

The prices of gas supplied to the domestic market have been inhibiting factors. Until recently they were set by a government decree and varied from $0.65 to $3.00 per mBtu. Pertamina, for example, could be ordered by the government to supply a fertilizer plant at the previously agreed price of $1.00 per mBtu despite this being likely to involve Pertamina in subsidizing the plant. A more realistic and freer price system may now be developing.

The state-owned distribution company, Perum Gas Negara (PGN), is now authorized not only as a gas distributor but also as a gas transmission company. It also intends to turn itself into a limited liability company with around 40 per cent of its shares taken by Pertamina and 20 per cent sold to private investors.[9] This new structure should enable it to undertake major capital projects and develop a broader and more dynamic domestic gas industry. There has been a certain amount of bureaucratic confusion between Pertamina and PGN. This, and more importantly the pricing situation, needs to be resolved before the government can develop and implement a cohesive domestic gas policy.

One of the main problems in providing more gas for domestic use is that the largest deposits of gas are far from Java, which holds more than two-thirds of the country's population and most of its industry.

Arco does have large oil and gas acreage offshore Java; the Kangean block, off the Island of Madura north of Bali in which BP holds a major stake and the North West Java Sea block, north and west of Java in which various independents also hold interests. Arco has long wanted to supply this gas to Java and the company has proved up substantial reserves and is hopeful that more will be discovered. The Offshore Northwest Java (ONJ) project was officially inaugurated in March 1994. The ONJ, operated by Arco, consists of a number of associated and small accumulations of gas gathered and brought ashore to supply two new power stations near Java. Another project inaugurated on the same day is a 430 km. pipeline, of which some 360 km. are undersea. This pipeline has been constructed to bring gas from the Kangean block to Gresik in East Java. Gas deliveries started in 1993 with eventual volumes of 600 million scf daily, making it the third largest pipeline in the world. This is the first significant project where a production-sharing contractor has developed a gas field for the domestic market. The price for Arco gas at the wellhead is currently put at $1.68 per tcf and $2.45 delivered onshore. Prices are related to field costs with no firm escalation clause in the contract.

Arco is operating a standard 20-year production-sharing contract with Pertamina and the gas is being sold on to downstream buyers, including the City of Surabaya for towns gas and to a fertilizer company. But the largest component of the additional gas sales will be PLN, the state electricity utility. PLN is building major gas-fired combined-cycle power plants at Tanjung Priok and Muara Karang near Jakarta and at Gresik near Surabaya, totalling 1.5GW. Eventually the new pipeline system could be linked to the system around Java.

Sumatran gas reserves are relatively remote and there have been plans to move the gas to Arco's North Western system. At present, however, the cheaper option of moving it from Asamera's holding in Sumatra north to Caltex's steam recovery project in the Duri oilfield seems more likely to be undertaken. Construction is due to start in 1996 of a line to Duri, backed by the Asian Development Bank. This stretch of the pipeline will be 540 km. long and an additional 283 km. of pipeline is also planned to run on to Batam Island for use by industry. This project is the most ambitious pipeline plan yet to be proposed in Indonesia. The vast and unexplored regions of eastern Indonesia may also contain sizeable gas reserves. If gas is proven up, then the modest infrastructure and small population of the east, would favour its use in fertilizer or methanol plants. It may also be an opportunity for conversion projects such as the Shell Middle Distillate Synthesis project (SMDS) recently put into operation in Malaysia. Considerable interest is being shown by the Indonesian government in the economics and practicality of the Malaysian project. If the SMDS plant proves successful it may well set the pattern for development in the more distant Indonesian gas fields.

The successful development of Indonesia's gas has, until now, been based on exports. Indonesia has been in the right place at the right time. It is ideally situated to supply the Japanese need for clean fuel and has made its gas available in substantial volumes well ahead of other suppliers. With the likelihood of substantial gas reserves yet to be proven up and with flexibility on the incentives needed to develop them, Indonesia will continue to play a major role in the South East Asian gas market well into the next century. In addition, with a realistic and clear policy for attracting the substantial downstream investment involved, particularly on prices, natural gas may also be able to replace oil as the main domestic source of energy.

## The Future for Gas

Important as the development of gas use for domestic consumption undoubtedly is, the sustaining and expansion of LNG exports is vital for the well-being of the nation.

Mobil produces all of the gas delivered to PT Arun for export and is currently making a major investment in compression facilities to bolster reservoir pressure. Reserves of gas in the Arun field, which started producing in 1971, are said to be running down and Mobil is actively looking for new replacement reserves in the area. The company is also engaged in a major gas exploration programme in a number of locations throughout Indonesia as well as contiguous to Arun.

Unocal, Total, and IJV (which includes LASMO, Union Texas and the Chinese Petroleum Corporation) are the principal suppliers to PT Badak, the 'non-profit making' operating company responsible for LNG operations at Bontang. Pertamina has a 55 per cent holding in the company itself, with Vico, Jilco and Total holding 20 per cent, 15 per cent and 10 per cent respectively. The facilities themselves are wholly owned by Pertamina.

All the supplying companies producing gas near the Badak plant pool their gas into a unified marketing effort and are remunerated according to their proportions of 'marketing packages'. These are based on the certified uncommitted reserves which each party has at the time the package is sold. The certification of reserves for Badak issued in May 1992 and based on the reserve position at the end of 1991, is shown in Table 4.7.

There are apparently about 175 bcm of reserves available to commit to future LNG marketing packages from Badak. This is roughly equivalent to 120 mt of LNG which would be adequate for additional contracts based on the new trains under construction and planned. The reserves are not by themselves adequate to enable existing major contracts to be extended. Table 4.7 also illustrates the growing influence of Total on supplies for Badak. This is based largely on its discovery of the major Peciko field with reserves in excess of 100 bcm. Interestingly, this field and other gas discoveries by Total are the result of a substantial exploration programme using the most modern techniques including 3-D seismic.

Whether enough reserves are available to secure rollovers or extensions is the major issue involved in the renewal of most of Indonesia's existing LNG contracts and the initiation of new ones. It is obviously in the government's interest to present a bullish view of what is available. The existing 1973 and 1981 contracts with Japanese interests for the supply of gas from both Badak and Arun were said to be backed by about 20 tcf of

**Table 4.7**:   East Kalimantan Gas Reserves and Badak LNG Sales Packages. Per Cent Share

| Package | *IJV* | *Total* | *Unocal* |
|---|---|---|---|
| | | *Per Cent Share* | |
| 1. (1973) 4.5 bcm | 97.9 | 2.1 | 0.0 |
| 2. (1981) 4.5 bcm | 66.4 | 29.2 | 4.4 |
| 3. (1987) 4.5 bcm | 29.6 | 45.6 | 24.8 |
| 4. (1990) 4.6 bcm | 25.0 | 65.0 | 10.0 |
| 5. (1996) n.a. | 25.0 | 72.0 | 3.0 |
| | | *Bcm* | |
| Certified Proven Reserves | 325 | 306 | 74 |
| Already Committed | 283 | 183 | 65 |
| Available for Sale | 42 | 123 | 9 |

Source: *World Gas Intelligence*, November 1992

reserves and there is supposedly an additional 20 tcf of committed reserves backing the other contracts. Even after taking into account the usually very substantial use in the field and by the LNG plants themselves, these would seem to be more than adequate to cover the life of existing contracts as Table 4.8 shows.

However, for Indonesia to assure its position as the leading LNG supplier well into the next century and to meet increasing domestic demand, new gas must be made available in substantial quantities. Although there are many possibilities for additional supplies, the development of the massive gas reserves near Natuna Island in the South China Sea is considered vital if future needs are to be adequately met. Conoco's Belida field in the Natuna Sea, which was inaugurated in 1993, already produces gas with its crude oil. The main Natuna field is said to contain some 41 per cent of Indonesia's current reserves of gas. Estimates of 210 tcf (5,900 bcm) of gas in place together with 45 tcf of recoverable hydrocarbons have been made. This would be equivalent to over 4,000 mt of LNG or 180 years of current annual exports.

Esso Indonesia, together with Pertamina, holds equal shares in the rights to develop 'Natuna D-Alpha block'. This field lies 225 km. north-east of Natuna Island. On conservative official estimates the block contains 28.7 tcf (790 bcm), equivalent to 570 mt of LNG. Unfortunately, the development of this field is complicated by the high $CO_2$ content of the gas, which is around 70 per cent. Exactly how the carbon dioxide will be handled

**Table 4.8:** Reserves Supporting LNG Contracts. LNG Equivalent in Million Tonnes

| | |
|---|---|
| Reserves Backing 1973/1981 Contracts (Badak/Arun) | 400 |
| Additional Reserves for Other Contracts (Badak/ Arun) | 400 |
| Total | 800 |
| | |
| Original Contracts     (7.5 for 23 Years) | 173 |
|                                       6.5 for 20 Years) | 130 |
| Other Existing Contracts | ca 100 |
| Total | 403 |

Source: *Gas Matters, Cedigaz News Report*

given the environmental concerns on releasing it to the atmosphere is not clear. The possibility of the $CO_2$ being injected into aquifers once it is separated from the saleable gas has been mentioned in this context. It is claimed that over 200 production wells and 18 offshore platforms will be necessary for full development of the Natuna gas project. Some $17 billion was estimated in 1991 to be required for its development, more than 40 per cent of which is needed for the technology to remove and dispose of the $CO_2$. Other estimates put total investment needs as high as $40 billion over a number of years for a potential production of 15 mt of LNG.

The need to deal with such unusually high levels of carbon dioxide has clearly made it a high-cost development. Technical costs of production are said to be around $2 to $2.5 per mBtu (1990 $) compared with well under $1 per mBtu for gas from Sumatra and Kalimantan. The Natuna project was stalled presumably because Exxon believes that the present contract arrangements with Pertamina make the investment uneconomic. Exxon has been negotiating with the government for the last two years or so to obtain more favourable fiscal terms within the PSC to compensate for the extraordinary and substantial capital costs required. It is thought that Exxon is holding out for a 50/50 split in revenue gas and an improvement in taxation terms. Presumably the new 55/45 split announced in 1992 for 'difficult' gas areas was intended to go some way to meeting this. It does now seem certain that Esso Natuna will be the operator and a basic agreement is due to be signed in 1995. The agreement is said to involve a 60/40 split of net final revenue in Pertamina's favour, with tax levied at 35 per cent. The government is also said to be having a first tranche share of gas valued in dollars before tax is applied.

It is unlikely that Pertamina will be able to raise the capital needed to fund its full share of the development costs. According to its president, it may therefore reduce its share in the field to around 10 per cent. A number of companies, including Nissho Iwai, Mitsui, Mitsubishi and Mobil have shown an interest in taking a part of the Pertamina share and its obligations, but any such arrangements have apparently yet to be agreed.

Pertamina proposed in 1990 that the Natuna reserves be linked by pipeline to the Arun terminal, thus supporting the construction of additional LNG trains at Arun. Another proposal, said to be favoured by Mobil and apparently the basis for the new agreement, is for an offshore LNG complex. Under this scheme, there would initially be two or three trains which would eventually be increased to six or more with a total production of around 15 mt. In theory deliveries could commence within eight years. There is also the possibility of converting additional gas to methanol or middle distillates on site. Other proposals had included moving the gas from Natuna through Sumatra and across the Straits of Sunda to Java or by pipeline across Kalimantan, picking up additional gas on the way to the existing Badak LNG plant. One dampener on these kind of schemes is the need for additional safety precautions in laying a line across the busy sea lanes that surround the archipelago.

Singapore was once targeted as a potential customer for Natuna gas. This possibility now seems less likely as Malaysia has signed an agreement to supply gas through the Trans-Malaysian trunk line system. It has recently been announced that PT Magna Primatara, a newly established private oil company and the Petroleum Authority of Thailand (PTT) signed a memorandum of understanding for a 25-year supply of 500 mcf/d of gas to Thailand from Natuna. This would reportedly be moved by a 700 km. pipeline to Thailand and used largely for power generation. This is supposed to involve a joint exploration venture by the two companies who will enter into a PSC with Pertamina for exploration in the Natuna Sea. This kind of agreement means very little without a clear indication of where the capital and expertise for the project is to come from and when it is actually planned to be in place.

There are many problems to be overcome – particularly on the way the financing is shared and the overall policy on gas use – before the Natuna field can be developed. The technical viability of Natuna and the possibility of supplies at a price acceptable to the potential customers remain major areas of doubt. However, what was once seen as completely unrealistic is increasingly being considered in concrete terms.

Certainly, a sense of urgency is needed if the project is to be put in place before rival supply projects for the Japanese market in Alaska and Sakhalin are developed. These sources are closer to Japan, giving freight cost advantages, and may also be capable of being developed more cheaply, although this is by no means sure.

The up-front costs of the project are the biggest hindrance to negotiations with possible purchasers and participants and an inevitably high base price is foreseen. As an additional sweetener to offering large shares in the equity, there is talk of supplies from Natuna being linked with access to existing cheaper sources, such as the output of a new train at Badak. There is certainly a need to reach a firm decision soon on the development of Natuna if it is to be seen as capable of being onstream by the turn of the century in time to influence the renegotiations of the current contracts with Japan.

As mentioned earlier, new measures were introduced in September 1992 as part of the overall oil and gas incentive package, to promote exploration for gas in both conventional and frontier areas. Contractors are allowed to retain a larger share of production. Positive steps towards more commercial and flexible pricing, in line with neighbouring Malaysia and Thailand and rivals for foreign investment, would also help to encourage investment in new domestic gas projects in Indonesia. It is hoped that the introduction of more realistic contractual terms will encourage the development of small local gas markets and perhaps innovatory techniques such as the use of floating methanol plants, particularly in the remote areas of eastern Indonesia.

There have been other gas discoveries in Northern Sumatra. One field, Kuala Langsa operated by Asamera and financed partly by a consortium headed by Japex, may have considerable potential. However, the size of the reserves involved is still uncertain. This and other discoveries could be fed into the existing facilities in Arun to support the extension and expansion of current contracts. Such discoveries could also help to build a substantial local market in Sumatra and on the potential boom island of Batam off Singapore. The existence of a market with the necessary supply infrastructure would also eventually provide local sales revenue that might improve the economics of Natuna.

A danger is that the development of smaller discoveries to feed into existing facilities may be seen as a more viable option than Natuna. Certainly if the discoveries are significant the development of the high-cost Natuna might be postponed. On the other hand the successful development of Natuna would provide just the confidence in the commercial future of Indonesia's gas industry that could stimulate massive gas activity throughout the archipeligo. A long-term aim is to interconnect a number of projects to form a trans-Indonesia gas pipeline system. This would connect North Sumatra with South Sumatra, Java, East Kalimantan and South Sulawesi.

Indonesia has many pipeline projects in the planning stage and even more in the conceptual stage.[10] There is no lack of interest in developing the country's still substantially untapped gas resources, although there is an impression of development being at the crossroads. It could continue through to the next century with a slow build-up of reserves, the completion of a few new pipeline projects and a steady increase in domestic gas use, especially on Java. On the other hand the pace of expansion throughout the archipelago could be extremely rapid. New pipelines breed new demand and the development of new fields and vice versa. Success in attracting investment might spiral the whole gas development process upwards. Gas could take over from oil by the end of the century as the major domestic fuel and gas exports capture a bigger share of world markets.

There are many opportunities in gas development around the world open to international investment funds and Indonesia has to compete for them. If it can at least match the terms available elsewhere and resolve any lingering bureaucratic difficulties, with continuing political stability the country will be able to achieve the progress in gas development that it needs.

## Notes

1. *Oil and Gas Journal*; estimated proved reserves at 1 April, 1994, 64,388 bcf. *World Oil*; reserves at end 1993, 67,532 bcf (reserves at end 1980, 28,935 bcf). *Petroleum Report of Indonesia*; proven reserves, 64.4 tcf, potential reserves, 37.2 tcf. *Cedigaz News Report*; recoverable reserves, 94 tcf (including 38 tcf in Natuna). Total resources, 217 tcf. Pertamina (April 1994); proven and probable, 114 tcf, total resource, 213 tcf.
2. One reservoir in the Natuna Sea, Natuna D Alpha is said to contain 210 tcf of raw gas, although a large fraction is of carbon dioxide. Natural gas has also been located in the West Natuna Sea. Markets are, as ever, the problem and the key to their development. *Indonesia: Source Book*, 1993.

3. Quoted in *Oil and Gas Journal*, 31 April, 1994.
4. Equity split for gas under 1992 package: existing and extended contract areas, 70/30 (in water depths of more than 1,500 metres, 60/40). New contract areas in conventional areas, 65/35, in frontier areas, 60/40 (in water depths of more than 1,500 metres, 55/45). Barrows Co. Inc., 1993.
5. Minister Ginandjar announced as part of his February 1989 incentives that gas prices would be oriented towards field development economics for new projects not approved or committed at that date. President Suharto at the official inauguration of the two pipeline projects on 5 March, 1994 said that his government would adjust its gas policy to encourage investors to explore for oil and gas reserves. He stated that Indonesia had discovered abundant reserves of natural gas but he called for more exploration to guarantee future supplies. *Gas Matters*, March 1994.
6. Japan is reported to have agreed in principle to extend the two 20-year contracts. The contract signed in 1973 would be extended for another ten years to 2009 covering 8.4 mt per annum. The 1981 contract would be extended for another five years to 2008 covering 3.6 mt per annum. Antara news agency quoted in *FT International Gas Report*, 18 February, 1994.
7. At the Indonesian Petroleum Congress of 1993. Quoted in *Gas Matters*, October 1993.
8. Ibid.
9. In accordance with Ministry of Mines and Energy decree No.785 KM PE/1992. Pertamina is apparently interested in purchasing up to 49% of the new company's shares. *Petroleum Report of Indonesia*, 1993.
10. Projects include: Asamera; Corridor block (S.Sumatra) to Duri with a spur to Batan. South Sumatra to N.W Java (Cilecon). N.Sumatra to Medan. S. Sumatra (from Asamera fields) to S. Sumatra (Pertamina's Prabumulih field). East Java (Surabaya) to West Java (Cilamaya). West Java (Arco, Maxus, JOLCO, and Pertamina fields) to onshore. East Java (from Mobil, Arco and Pertamina). Central Java (from Shell offshore fields). East Kalimantan (from Unocal, Pertamina fields) to Balikpapan and Samarinda. South Sulawesi (from BP fields) to Ujung Pandang. *Petroleum Report of Indonesia, Gas Matters, Indonesian Development Quarterly*, various issues.

# 5   MORE ENERGY SOURCES:
## THE ALTERNATIVES

Indonesia is a country fortunate to have substantial and diverse energy resources. It clearly makes sense for any country to develop the full range of its resources providing they are economically feasible and that a sensible balance can be struck between needs and availability.

Although oil and gas play the major role in Indonesia's current energy economy and are likely to do so for many years to come, the country has an abundance of other energy resources. Some, such as coal and hydroelectricity, are already being developed apace; others, such as peat, nuclear power and modern renewables are still waiting in the wings.

## Coal

As in many other countries, coal was once an important source of energy for a range of uses for power generation and in industry and railways. Despite strenuous efforts by the government in the post-war period to revive production it never rose above half the level of 1.8 mt achieved in 1939. By 1962, annual production had fallen to 0.5 mt because of transport problems, labour difficulties and lack of spare parts. Through the 1970s and early 1980s production and domestic consumption remained at around this level.

The 1970s brought a revival of interest in coal around the world and some of this was reflected in Indonesia. A presidential instruction issued in 1976 called for the development of coal supplies to provide an alternative domestic source of energy to oil. Its main use would be for power generation. A substantial part of the government's energy planning during the early 1980s was devoted to considering and encouraging the development prospects for coal. The World Bank and some major international energy companies were involved and the usual studies by outside consultants proliferated.

Certainly a great deal of effort and hard currency were spent to expand and improve the production of indigenous coal and to develop potential markets. Current energy policy still views increased domestic use of coal as a key way of reducing pressure on oil supplies and the expansion of coal exports as a valuable source of hard currency. Unfortunately, coal has never had the political clout of oil and progress has been, until relatively recently, desperately slow.

The resource base for solid fuels in Indonesia is very substantial with the whole spectrum of quality available, ranging from peat to anthracite. The majority of the country's coal consists, however, of low grade lignite with a high moisture content. Estimates of the size of reserves vary widely from 4.2 billion tonnes to over 32 billion tonnes.[1] The World Energy Council has indicated proved recoverable reserves of bituminous coal of some 962 mt with some 7,100 of sub-bituminous and 24,000 mt of lignite.[2]

In practice, such national reserves estimates are incomplete and are usually out of date and unreliable. Taken as a whole, they probably have very little real significance.[3] One attraction of Indonesian coal is that much of it is found in large seams in sedimentary basins which allow relatively easy open-cast mining. Most of the bituminous coal currently being mined is located in South Sumatra and South Kalimantan. It is a good quality coal with a low sulphur content and a generally low level of ash (around 1 per cent). Its heating value is in the range 26 to 34 MJ per Kg.

Between 1978 and 1985 the government encouraged foreign investors to enter into production-sharing contracts for the exploration and production of coal. This resulted in the granting of 30-year concessions in East and West Kalimantan to ten foreign contractors. The difficulty in attracting investment in new coal facilities was recognized by the terms of the contracts. Under these, a substantial 86.5 per cent of any coal produced is taken by the contractor with the remainder going to one of the two state-owned coal companies. There are, however, provisions for the eventual sale of up to 51 per cent of the business to Indonesian interests. There are now 11 private coal contractors from a range of countries engaged in mining operations in Indonesia. The two state-owned companies merged in October 1990 to form P.T. TBBA (Tambang, Batubara, Bukit Asam) in a move designed to cut costs and improve efficiency in the state mines. There are also a number of small mine operations owned by local Indonesian private companies or village cooperatives.

The bout of exploration activity in the 1980s duly led to the discovery of worthwhile deposits and the largest, in East Kalimantan, is able to support production at over 2 mt per annum. All the export oriented mines planned for Kalimantan have access to the coast without the need to construct major rail facilities.

Coal has been mined from the Ombilin and Bukit Asam coalfields on Sumatra for many years under primitive conditions. In recent years there has been an extensive programme of upgrading and renovating the existing mines and transport facilities on both fields. New PSCs to further exploit Ombilin were signed in 1985 with foreign and joint venture companies. Coal from the underground mines at Ombilin is exported to a number of South East Asian countries as well as being used by three domestic cement works. The development of the Bukit Asam coalfield, managed by the state-owned mining corporation, has also been encouraged in order to provide fuel for the large new Suralaya power station on West Java as well as for a power station at the mine itself. This work was financed largely by the World Bank. Unfortunately, progress on the mine was slower than planned so that foreign coal had to be imported for the power stations.

Despite considerable prevarication, mistakes and delays in the past, the coal programme has been successful and production is now growing rapidly. There are six active coal mines in the country as a whole. While coal production in the early 1980s was under 0.4 mt per annum, by 1985 it had risen to 1.5 mt although Indonesia remained a net importer of coal until 1988. By 1993, production had climbed to a substantial 27 mt, approximately 56 per cent of which is produced by foreign contractors; 17 mt were exported. Annual output is believed to have reached over 30 mt by 1995 and is officially expected, rather hopefully, to be over 60 mt by the end of the century.

Most coal produced from Bukit Asam, Ombilin and the smaller mines has been used for domestic purposes although there are some exports of anthracite. The main domestic users are the cement and other mineral industries and especially power generation which is the fastest growing outlet and the main stimulus for the construction of the domestically oriented mines.

The price of coal to domestic consumers has been heavily subsidized in order to compete with the subsidized price of fuel oil. Nevertheless, coal still only supplies some 6 per cent of total Indonesian domestic demand for commercial energy. The decision in the 1993/94 budget to eliminate subsidies for oil fuel should encourage more use of coal by households and small industries. The government has for some time planned to develop the use of coal briquettes as a substitute for kerosene and fuel wood and production began in 1993. The aim is a 30 per cent penetration of the household sector and 50 per cent of small industries by 1998. Domestic sales of coal have increased at around 5 per cent per annum and are projected to rise to 27 mt by the end of Pelita 5.[4] Nonetheless, these targets are extremely ambitious and will be difficult to achieve, not least because of popular demand for the more efficient and 'modern' hydrocarbon based fuels. Additional demand from household and other potential domestic users will be of help in constraining oil needs but is unlikely to be of major significance to the overall energy balance.

Much of the drive for new coal facilities comes from the need to substitute for the use of fuel oil for power generation and to broaden the fuel base because of the expected decline or, at best, stagnation in crude oil production. PLN, the state utility, already generates some 25 per cent of its electricity from coal, with 55 per cent as the target for 1999 and 66 per cent by 2004. There may well be conflict here with the latest policies on gas-fired power generation and the privatization of electricity generation. Nonetheless, substantial increases in production will be required. Some 3.8 GW of major coal-fired generating plant was planned for construction in various parts of Indonesia by the end of 1995 on top of the existing 1.7 GW. By the end of the century, it is hoped to have 10 GW in place which could mean demand for an additional 20 mt of coal per annum. This seems feasible although much of this increase is dependent on attracting private investment for the generating plant.

A desire to become a major player in the expanding international coal market and to open up a new source of foreign exchange earnings has also been a major driving force behind the expansion in coal production. There are currently two coal export ports at Balikpapan on Borneo and at Tanjung Bara on

Kalimantan with a rated capacity of 2.5 and 7 mt respectively. An additional export port with a capacity of 8 mt is planned at Pulau Laut. Another port at Tarahan on South Sumatra is geared to supplying the Suralaya power station with coal from Bukit Asam.

Out of a total Indonesian coal production of approximately 27 mt in 1993, 17 mt were exported, generating over $700 million. Exports are believed to be increasing still and Indonesia has already passed Colombia to become the world's fourth largest coal exporter. The bulk of exports is from mines operated by international contractors. The target under the Plan was once for production to reach 15 mt in 1993/94. This now looks to have been a serious underestimation of what was actually achievable with the help of foreign contractors. Exports have been forecast to reach some 25 to 30 mt by the end of the 1990s. On this basis and with increased domestic demand for power generation, coal production would have to reach 40 to 50 mt by the turn of the century. Although this level of production and exports would be feasible in terms of port capacity and of the resource base,[5] realities of the international market for steam coal may make such forecasts for export sales somewhat optimistic.

The main market for Indonesia's coal lies in the Pacific Rim countries although there are exports to Europe. Many of these countries are pushing ahead with other sources for power generation, particularly gas, and seem less interested in coal than they used to be. In addition, Australia is a major competitor for Indonesian coal in the Japanese and other markets. Indonesian export coal has a slightly lower calorific value than some of the Australian coals that it competes with but in other respects it can be of comparable quality and does seem to have an advantage on cost (see Table 5.1).

Australian steam coal from New South Wales with a calorific value of around 28 GJ per tonne can be delivered to Japan at a full cost of $35 to $55 per tonne. Indonesian steam coal was being delivered to Japan at $25 to $35 per tonne for a somewhat lower calorific value. Although such comparisons without full quality details and on an indicative basis can be misleading it does seem that Indonesian coal has a cost advantage over its main competitor.

**Table 5.1:** Indicative Costs of Indonesian Export Steam Coal. $ Per Tonne. (Calorific Value 26.4 GJ Per Tonne)

| | |
|---|---|
| Mine Operations | 8.5 (8–12) |
| Capital | 8.0 |
| Rail and Loading | 8.5 |
| f.o.b. (Operating Only) | 17.0 |
| f.o.b. (Full Costs) | 25.0 (22–28) |
| Freight to Japan | 12.0 (6–16) |
| c.i.f. Total (Operating) | 29.0 |
| c.i.f. Total | 37.0 (28–44) |

Source: IEA, *Coal Information*, 1992

One doubt over increasing supplies of coal for exports and domestic use is the ability of mine capacity and the infrastructure to expand sufficiently and on time. Official plans still exist for coal production to increase to as much as 60 mt by the end of the century and to 75 mt per annum a few years later. The construction of a large coal export and import centre at Batam Island off Singapore is also planned. Such levels of production are more than that of the UK at the moment and will probably be higher than German and UK production together in a few years. The level of additional production envisaged by the year 2000 would, on a straight replacement basis, obviate the need for an additional 700,000 b/d of oil products, thus considerably improving the availability of oil for export.

Coal pricing policy in relation to oil is crucial to increased oil substitution in the domestic market, but this has not yet been confronted. The further expansion of mine and port facilities depends largely on whether adequate foreign and particularly private capital can be attracted. The omens are not good. There is a glut of export coal capacity worldwide which will continue for some years to come. This is largely the result (as was the case for Indonesia) of development plans being made at a time when the coal market and prices to be obtained appeared more favourable to new investment. There are also more attractive opportunities for scarce international capital in other energy related fields.

Thus, although the more ambitious targets for Indonesian coal must be open to some doubt, the achievements of the past five years or so have been remarkable. Production levels of around 50 mt per annum by the end of the century seem feasible; any further contribution at acceptable costs that would free more oil for export, will be welcome to the economy.

## Hydropower

The exploitation of water resources for the generation of hydro electricity has long been a major objective of Indonesian energy policy. An archipelago clearly has advantages in terms of water supply, but there are disadvantages for developing a high voltage grid system that would enable hydro use across the country to be optimized. Most of Indonesia's islands have potential hydro sites although it is mainly on Java that the bulk of capacity has actually been built. Perhaps as much as 80 per cent of the possible economic sites has already been harnessed on Java and, unfortunately, it is here that the need for additional power is greatest. Thus, it is largely to the other islands that future expansion must turn. Kalimantan, Irian Jaya and Sumatra together have nearly 75 per cent of the remaining sites for power generation.

Although the theoretical capability is much higher, the overall technically usable potential for Indonesia as a whole is probably approximately 120 GW.[6] Perhaps one-third of this is exploitable in practical economic terms representing a potential displace-ment of oil or other fossil fuels of nearly 1 mb/d. At present around 7 GW of hydro capacity is actually in place, representing only 18 per cent of what could be done countrywide.

The state electricity utility (PLN), which is currently gener-ating around 20 per cent of its electricity from hydro, has ambitious plans to develop the available resources further. This makes sound economic sense given the many advantages of hydro when an adequate power load is available. In Java this is the case but elsewhere there is usually a need to develop a substantial industrial load before major investment can be justified. With most of the best sites already developed, it will be difficult to meet incremental electricity demand in Java from hydro unless underwater high voltage links are established with Sumatra. Unfortunately, this could double the investment required.

The initial investment needed for hydro plants is generally much greater than for comparable fossil fuelled plant.[7] Construction times are longer but fuel and other operational costs are negligible and, combined with a longer life, hydro is usually the cheapest source of base load electricity. Successful schemes on Sumatra and Kalimantan and elsewhere could, apart from the benefits to land usage, act as catalysts for economic development. They are, however, competing for scarce funds with coal-fired projects and, increasingly, with gas-fired projects whose capital costs are at least a quarter of those for hydro.

An additional difficulty is that many of the existing Indonesian hydro plants were built on the back of funding from lending institutions such as the World Bank. Many projected large-scale hydro schemes are now somewhat out of favour with these institutions, partly on environmental grounds, and funds are hard to come by. Certainly, the days of substantial financial support for the more grandiose projects seem to be over. It will also be difficult to attract private funds for hydro schemes because of the high up-front investment required and the long lead times compared with other power sources.

At present there is some 1.4 GW of hydroelectric capacity under construction and another 1.5 GW in the planning stages. This effort, although representing a substantial investment and certainly helping with the need to increase overall generating capacity by up to 10 GW before the end of the century, is not very significant within the context of the overall energy economy. It will displace less than 60,000 b/d of oil or other fuels. Some effort is also being put into the installation of small-scale hydro plants to displace local diesel generators although their impact on the country's energy needs will be minimal.

### Geothermal

As a result of its position on the crosspoint of two volcanic belts, Indonesia is rich in geothermal resources. Java alone has more than 100 volcanic cones of which 15 are currently active. Recent studies claim that some 217 sites throughout the country are, in aggregrate, theoretically capable of supplying about 16 GW of electricity generating capacity by using geothermal energy.[8] This could displace some 400,000 b/d of diesel fuel.

Other estimates talk of a somewhat lower potential of 3 to 10 GW of potential generating capacity.[9]

The concentration of geothermal in Indonesia has, in the past, aroused a deal of interest, particularly amongst various international bodies and others keen to conduct studies. Obviously, the geothermal potential of Indonesia represents an asset that should be developed where economical and where outlets exist. However, many of the fields are small, in isolated areas and at high altitude and require new infrastructure before they can be developed. There is also the problem of their economics in relation to other sources of electricity and heat. The cost effectiveness of geothermal varies very widely from location to location and is by no means as certain as the protagonists maintain. There is also a certain amount of divided responsibility and tension over geothermal between Pertamina and PLN which may have hampered development in the past. Pertamina is responsible for geothermal exploration and production and PLN is responsible for the generation and distribution of the electricity. Other parties, including foreign investors, may cooperate with Pertamina in developing geothermal facilities. Pertamina either develops a project directly and sells steam to PLN or a facility is developed under a joint operating contract (JOC) with private companies. Under the JOC, the contractor is the supplier to Pertamina but Pertamina remains the seller to PLN.

Positive steps to develop geothermal were first taken as long ago as 1973 with the securing of a grant and technical assistance from the New Zealand government for the development of a 30 MW power plant at Kamojang. This has now been expanded to a capacity of 140 MW and remains the largest in operation. Pertamina has enlisted the help of several other foreign partners and a number of other small plants have been built or are under construction. However, a lot of the remaining potential sites are unlikely to prove attractive to outside investors or contractors not motivated by considerations of national prestige. Geothermal should be able to make a modest localized contribution to Indonesia's energy needs but it will never be more than a miniscule source of additional energy on a national scale.

## Nuclear Power

Another, potentially much more significant, source of additional
energy is nuclear. There has long been an interest in developing
the industry in Indonesia even though the base electricity load
has not until recently been adequate to support a nuclear power
plant. Some of the interest may have stemmed from military
considerations in the past, and indeed this may still be true.[10]

After many years of research and numerous studies on the
feasibility of using nuclear power to supplement its power needs,
more concrete plans are now in progress. Research reactors
and a plant for the production of fuel elements have been in
place since the 1980s. The National Atomic Energy Board
(Batan), under the auspices of the National Energy Coordinating
Board has been charged with the long-term task of overseeing
the construction of seven to twelve nuclear power plants. Units,
which are likely to be between 0.6 and 1.2 GW, are supposedly
set to come on line over a 12-year period although the actual
timing of construction is not clear.

Indonesia has a moderate potential for uranium and Batan,
which has the exclusive rights, is actively exploring in much of
the country. Uranium has already been discovered some years
ago at various sites on Sumatra, Java, Sulawesi and Irian Jaya.
Although the quality is variable, there were plans in the 1970s
to use natural gas to process and enrich the uranium with
German assistance.

The first nuclear plant has long been planned for Mount
Muria on Central Java, 440 km. east of Java, which arouses
some disquiet because of its volcanic location. There has been
something of a stop–go policy on this project which is connected
with the waxing and waning of the influence of advocates of
economic growth based on technological revolution. Nonetheless, there are still plans to build an 0.6 GW reactor costing
at least $1 billion. In March 1993, the government approved a
permit for the construction of a 1.2 GW plant at Paiton in East
Java. This will be a joint venture, made up of a consortium of
foreign companies and an Indonesian concern. General Electric
is involved as is Mitsui and the Export/Import Banks of Japan
and the USA have agreed to extend credit lines amounting to
$1.6 billion. It was hoped to call for tenders early in 1995, to

start construction in 1997 and to be producing electricity from nuclear power by 2004. This does seem a much firmer step than those previously taken although actual timing and even execution must be a little uncertain.

With the enormous amount of spare manufacturing capacity in the world nuclear industry, Indonesia must have come under a lot of selling pressure in recent years from organizations desperate to keep their operations going. For full electrification to the levels required for a newly industrializing country, Indonesia will certainly need to instal substantial amounts of generating capacity, perhaps having to add some 30 GW by the year 2010. Nuclear is an option to meet some of this increment but it is one which is fraught with problems as, for example, India and the Philippines can testify. Not the least of these involve cost overruns, lengthy delays in completions and technical operating problems. On the other hand South Korea has managed to achieve a successful nuclear programme and there is no reason why Indonesia cannot do the same, given tight and technically orientated direction.

Whether it might not be better to give priority for scarce funds and expertise to gas development and gas-powered combined-cycle plants or to the further development of low sulphur coal is something which must be exercising the minds of the National Energy Coordinating Board and PLN.

## Other Energy Sources

As part of its policy of diversifying energy sources, the government has experimented with numerous unconventional technologies and sources of energy. Solar power projects have been implemented quite successfully in remote islands where electricity is costly to provide by conventional means. PLN has recently completed a $1.65 million pilot scheme to provide 3,000 homes with solar panels. There has also been some work on wind power and on the use of thermal gradients in the ocean as well as large-scale solar applications. Most of these projects have one thing in common, namely a high cost in comparison with more conventional forms of energy. The Indonesian policy has been cautious and one feels that, very sensibly, the government has no desire to allow the country to become a testing ground for others. In any case the impact of solar systems on overall energy supply, for example, using presently available technology can only be small.

Indonesia possesses the fourth largest peat resources in the world although they are barely exploited at present. Estimates of the amount available vary so widely as to be almost meaningless. A modest estimate might be 60 billion boe, equivalent to 100 years of crude oil at current production levels. Unfortunately, there are a number of factors likely to restrain early exploitation. The main drawback is the low calorific value of peat which gives high transport and distribution costs and makes it uncompetitive against competing fuels. Most major industries able to use solid fuel or planning to do so are already near the coalfields. A number of private companies have shown interest in establishing a pilot power plant project based on peat.[11] However, given the very substantial resources of coal that are available and the competition for development funds from other higher quality resources, peat is not likely to play a significant role for many years to come, if ever.

Although there are considerable resources of biomass in the form of logging and agricultural waste and in primary forests, there seems little enthusiasm for new ways of using the biomass as a fuel. There are some plans for ethanol production and a logical route, in view of the high-level middle distillate demand, would be the production of diesel fuel from vegetable sources. As with peat, the abundance of conventional energy sources that can be used more easily and efficiently is a barrier to the development of fuels from biomass. There are other barriers such as social and land ownership patterns but the logistics and particularly the economics act negatively. These barriers will not prevent localized contributions but the effect on overall energy supplies and particularly oil demand seems likely to be minimal.

To conclude, this is really the case for most of the alternative energy resources to oil and gas in Indonesia's extensive armoury. Coal is already a major source of export earnings and is carving a niche in the domestic market. Of the others, only hydro and, perhaps, nuclear possess realistic prospects of being of any real significance. Of course any major industrializing country needs continually to consider the energy alternatives open to it.

However, it would seem sensible for scarce resources of capital and technical and management ability to be concentrated on tried and cost effective oil, gas and coal. If the development of these three is adequately encouraged and coordinated, the country will have an abundance of energy for export and domestic use for many years to come.

## Notes

1. Economist Intelligence Unit *Country Profile*, 1992. *Petroleum Report of Indonesia*, 1990.
2. Only about 10 per cent of the country's area has been surveyed and, in any case, what is actually meant by coal 'reserves' is often not clear nor are the classifications consistent.
3. *Indonesia: Source Book*, 1993 puts known coal reserves at an estimated 34 billion tonnes, of which 18 billion tonnes are on Sumatra. *Green Energy Matters*, December 1991, put measured reserves of medium to high quality, low and medium sulphur coal at over 28 billion tonnes.
4. Pelita 5 ends in 1999. *Indonesia: Source Book*, 1993.
5. Kalimantan should have the capacity to ship as much as 40 mt per annum in Pannamax vessels or larger by the end of 1994. The new terminals being built are necessary if Indonesian coal is to compete in Europe. The rapid loading of Cape sized vessels is probably necessary to obtain the most advantageous freight rates for long hauls. World Bank, *Steam Coal for Power in Indonesia: Issues and Scenarios*.
6. *International Water Power and Dam Construction*, 1992.
7. Capital costs can range from $1,500 to $4,000 per kW for hydro compared with, for example, a gas-fired combined-cycle power plant of $400 to $600 per kW. *OIES Review of Energy Costs*, 1991.
8. About half the total capacity is on Java. *Indonesia: Source Book*, 1993.
9. *Survey of Energy Resources*, World Energy Council.
10. Much of the pressure for a nuclear programme has come from the technologists led by Dr. Habibie, who has said that Indonesia cannot rely merely on natural resources for electricity generation. Critics have expressed concerns about the high development costs involved and the possible environmental impact. *Petroleum Report of Indonesia*, 1991. Another reason for pushing nuclear may be the feeling that all energy technologies should be exploited in the country. As Vice-President Sudharmono has said: 'Almost every source of energy which can serve mankind has been utilised in this country. Only nuclear energy has not been used.' *Asian Energy Review*, April 1994.
11. Bids were made by five companies during 1993 for the construction of a 100 MW power plant at Pontianak in West Kalimantan. *Jakarta Post*, 29 March, 1993.

# 6 THE MEANS TO THE END: POLICY, PERTAMINA AND THE ORGANIZATION OF THE OIL AND GAS SECTOR

## The Underlying Policies

Indonesia has by far the largest population of all the OPEC countries; the lowest income per head except for Nigeria; and its reserves of oil, its capacity to produce and its revenues are all small in relation to most other members of OPEC.[1] In these circumstances and with over 3 million people being added to the population each year, the country has had little real choice on practical policy. It has to maximize the production of oil and gas in order to generate capital for development and to satisfy domestic demand for energy.

However, there are other much more favourable contrasts with the majority of OPEC members. Indonesia has very large and varied mineral and agricultural resources that are being actively and successfully exploited. It also now has a substantial and rapidly growing manufacturing sector with considerable export potential. In addition, there is a full range of alternative energy sources available within its borders; it is the world's largest exporter of liquefied natural gas and coal is already a contributor to foreign exchange earnings. To crown these advantages, Indonesia has a strategic location in what is, arguably, the world's most economically dynamic region. It also has an enterprising population with a sound leavening of competent technocrats in government.

The ultimate aim for energy policy must be for national income to rise to levels sufficient to provide an adequacy of domestic savings so that growth can be generated without further excessive dependence on oil and gas revenues. Indonesia has indeed had considerable success in ensuring that the depletion of its oil and gas resources is matched by growth in real capital assets and there has been substantial diversification of the economy.[2] Nonetheless, dependence on revenues from oil and gas remains high.

A central and constant theme of energy policy since the country's independence in 1945 has been the need for the state to own the oil and gas reserves and to exercise full control over their development. Article 33 of the 1945 Constitution states: 'Branches of production which are important to the state and which affect the life of the people, shall be controlled by the state ... land and water and the natural resources therein shall be controlled by the state and shall be exploited for the greatest welfare of the people.'

During the 1950s and 1960s, the gathering of control by the state over all aspects of the oil and gas industry was successfully pursued. Indeed, there seemed to be an impression during this time that complete state control of the energy sector was the panacea for almost all the problems of the broader economy. Energy policy seemed to flow from that view. This was not, of course, a uniquely Indonesian attitude and it was during that period common to both old industrialized countries as well as post-colonial countries.

The takeover by the army of the North Sumatran fields in 1957 was followed by the introduction of Oil Mining Law No. 44 in 1960. This specified unambiguously that the mining of oil and gas should be undertaken by the state and carried out solely by a state enterprise. This, together with the revoking of the concession rights of the foreign oil companies, was a major milestone in the policy of state control of the oil and gas industry. By the time the contracts of work were signed by Caltex, Stanvac and Shell in 1963 and their concessions relinquished, Indonesia was master of its own oil and gas with state-owned companies firmly in place. Refining and marketing were made a monopoly of the national oil company and, in practice, their control became more absolute than for upstream activities.

Clearly in the early days of independence, the government had little choice other than to continue the contracts for the three international oil companies. Despite the strong wish to reduce foreign dependence, oil was far too important a source of revenue to take over immediately when there was no adequate national capability. The introduction of the work contract and subsequently the production-sharing contract was designed to bolster and maintain government ownership and control of hydrocarbon resources and production facilities and give the government a greater role in the management of the production process. In practice, under the work contracts, the government could neither exercise management control nor claim more than

20 per cent of its profit share in terms of oil supplies. The introduction of the PSC went much further in serving government interests by increasing ownership, management, revenues and operational control over operations. Recent years have seen only a modicum of softening on the question of equity participation by private companies for oil and gas development; much less than in other fields of activity.[3]

The central role of the state is obvious in the contractual arrangements for oil and gas development and the activities of Pertamina. In order to attract foreign investment, there has been some relaxation in policy towards foreign companies in other key industries, with deregulation and privatization. However, the government still retains the central role in all aspects of the energy economy. State enterprise has been, and still is, considered as integral to Indonesia's hydrocarbon policies. It continues to be seen as the most suitable way of providing the government with direct profits and control and of expanding the productive capacity of the industry. The various other arrangements for allowing foreign participation in the oil and gas business, as described in earlier chapters, offer only some minor relaxation of the full state monopoly. It is to be expected that any tempering of dogma to the practicalities of attracting scarce investment and skills, is unlikely to move rapidly for oil and gas. A strong nationalistic ethos exists among all strata of the population and in most parts of the country and this is firmly linked to oil and gas. Understandably, this is not something that any Indonesian government would or could go against unless it were well disguised. Thus, a visible expression of the state's ownership and control will always remain of paramount importance however much flexibility is introduced beneath the surface.

The first detailed expression of energy policy in terms of targets for investment in energy and for hydrocarbon production, refinery output and so on was used as input for the Third Five-Year Plan (1979–84). Basic policy has remained the same through subsequent Plans although the emphasis and the means used to implement policy has shifted, from time to time, in response to internal and external pressures. Nevertheless, the Plans still contain detailed targets for oil and gas.

A major policy objective is to move from a single- to a multi-energy based economy. This involves strengthening the position of exportable energy sources, largely oil and gas but also coal, as foreign exchange earners, while simultaneously developing non-exportable energy sources to support the economy and the wider plans for the future well-being of the country.

The recently concluded Five-Year Plan (1 April, 1989 to 31 March, 1994), in common with earlier ones, had targets for a gradual reduction in the share of domestic energy demand met from oil and an increase in the contribution of natural gas, coal, hydroelectricity, geothermal and other renewables. The encouragement of energy conservation is also a part of policy but one which does not always seem to be too seriously addressed.

The maintenance of an aggressive exploration and development programme for oil and gas is an obvious part of any Indonesian national energy policy. The expansion and optimization of refining capabilities to support growing product demand and reduce the middle distillate deficit is another key element. Underlying such a commonsense national energy policy, and sometimes acting as a hindrance to it, is the need to keep a rapidly growing and potentially explosive population content. This includes the provision of a ready supply of relatively cheap basic fuels.

In the domestic market, Indonesia has long followed a cheap oil policy. Together with a high rate of economic growth, this has been largely responsible for oil consumption growing at very high rates in the past. Low fuel oil and diesel prices, especially against a background of high inflation, have also discouraged coal production and damaged the fuelwood and charcoal industries (the latter exacerbating rural unemployment). There has in addition been a more general misallocation of resources through low fuel prices. For example, low fares based on low fuel costs encouraged demand for public transport that could not be fulfilled. However, the situation has now changed significantly. Subsidies on products have been reduced in recent years, from the 6 to 8 per cent of domestic revenues in the early 1980s to about 2 to 3 per cent of domestic revenues in 1992. Most of the remaining subsidies on domestic fuels were eliminated in 1993 and should all be removed by 1999.

Kerosene was the most heavily supported oil product with diesel and fuel oil also being subsidized, but not gasoline. The price of kerosene is still very sensitive politically as it is the main commercial cooking fuel in lower income households. Previous attempts to raise kerosene prices by significant amounts have met with vigorous street protests, but the most recent move to bring it up to market prices indicates a certain political confidence within an improved economic climate. The removal of subsidies on diesel fuel and kerosene should help to restrain the burgeoning middle distillate imbalance.

The contractual arrangements for oil and gas exploration and development have also undergone changes away from blanket state control and ownership. As described earlier, the pre-eminent legal form for exploration and development of oil and gas is the production-sharing contract. In recent years a whole variety of different and often flexible arrangements have been introduced, mainly to encourage activity in offshore or remote areas or in enhanced oil recovery.

It seems to be well recognized by the Indonesian government that there is an increasing need to show more flexibility in terms for participation in both upstream and downstream activities; the last six years have seen four sets of major revisions to the PSCs. There may now be much more willingness to move from the old rigidity although, so far, this has stopped short of real equity sharing in upstream activities. Indonesia's relations with the international oil industry and in particular the majors are less prickly and confrontational than in the past. There is a much stronger feeling of self-confidence on the government's part and more awareness of the realities of international business and market. Nonetheless, it still appears reluctant to take bolder steps in order to attract the large-scale investment that is needed for oil and gas.

There will always be the political need for the government to be seen to be maintaining its sovereignty over oil and gas activities. However, behind the outward form, we may well see over the next few years substantial changes developing in the relationship between government and the companies.

## Organization of the Energy Sector

*Overall Structure.* In addition to its basic governmental functions, the Ministry of Mines and Energy has prime control over energy

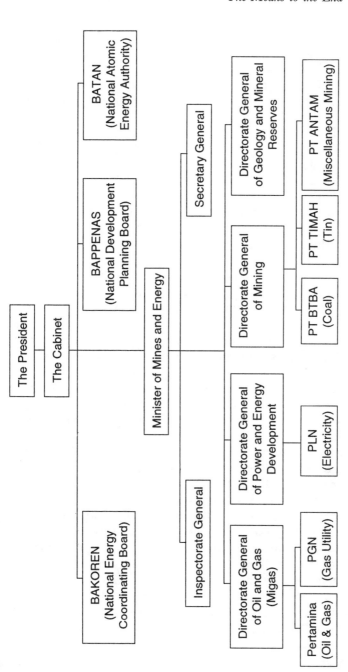

**Figure 6.1:** Organization of the Energy Industry

activities through four Directorates General. One is responsible for mines and mineral resources including coal; a second is responsible for oil and gas; a third for electric power, other energy resources and policy integration; a fourth is responsible for geological activities. A number of state enterprises come directly under the ministry, including P.T. TBBA for the state coal mines, PLN for electricity, PGN the state gas utility and Pertamina.

Within the Ministry, the Directorate General of Oil and Gas (Migas) has primary responsibility for oil and gas and oversees the activities of Pertamina.[4] This supervisory role as it affects Pertamina's relations with foreign contractors is mainly concerned with ensuring that the companies comply with the relevant Indonesian laws such as foreign exchange regulations, land use, and so forth. Migas also includes Lemnigas, the Indonesian oil and gas research and tecnnological development organization which monitors crude oil and product specifications. The Indonesian Oil and Gas Academy is also operated by Migas. A National Energy Coordinating Board (Bakoren) endeavours to pull together the potentially conflicting activities of the Energy Ministry and other ministries and bodies with an involvement in managing energy resources. Bakoren was established by a presidential decree in August 1980 to establish a comprehensive and integrated energy policy and to coordinate its implementation. It is basically a forum for the consideration of major energy decisions, particularly domestic energy use and pricing. The Energy Resources Technical Committee (PTE) formulates national energy plans and provides assistance and recommendations to the Board on energy matters. Bakoren is a non-structural coordinating body reporting directly to the Cabinet and chaired by the Minister of Mines and Energy. The Board includes, amongst others, the President Director of Pertamina as well as the Ministers of Defence and Industry and the Chairman of the National Development Planning Board (Bappenas). The Minister of Mines and Energy is also the Chairman of Bakoren, and is thus the leading Indonesian government spokesman on energy policy matters. Policy decisions relating to pricing, production volumes and relations with contractors are initiated by or require the concurrence of the minister and his agreement before implementation. The minister is also the head of the Indonesian delegation to OPEC meetings.

Another important influence on energy policy is the State Minister for Research and Technology and Chairman of the Agency for the Assessment and Application of Technology (BPPT). The holder of this position is B.J. Habibie who has long been an advocate of large-scale technically advanced projects such as nuclear power and has significantly influenced the type of fuel to be used for electricity generating.

*Pertamina.* The main instrument of government policy and activity in the oil and gas sector is Pertamina, the state oil and gas company. It has a long history stemming from the early takeovers by workers' unions and by the army during the fight for independence. It has been no stranger to controversy throughout much of its history.

Between 1957 and 1961, the government formed three national oil companies, Permigan, Pertamin and Permindo, in order to assert its control of oil and gas resources and to create a nationally-owned oil and gas industry.[5] In 1968, Permindo was eliminated and the two remaining nationally-owned energy companies were merged to form a single wholly state-owned firm, PN Pertamina.[6] The new company was made accountable to the Ministry of Mines and Energy but its leadership was chosen from the army, who also benefited indirectly from its finances. Its first President Director was the redoubtable Dr Ibnu Sutowo. Pertamina was originally subject to the provisions of a law passed in 1960 when the state oil company was a relatively small concern contributing only modestly to the national income. Law No. 8 of 1971 established a new corporation, Pertamina, in place of the old one.[7] It is now Indonesia's largest industrial enterprise and still possesses the sole rights to almost all activities throughout the oil and gas sector. Law No. 8 outlined the framework within which the company could take part in non oil and gas activities but, in practice, there was considerable leeway available to make non-hydrocarbon investments.

Pertamina explores for and produces oil on its own account, arranges all foreign oil and gas contracts and supervises the activities of the domestic and foreign contractors. It is also charged with supplying oil products to the domestic market and has a near monopoly over fuel distribution. Through subsidiary and joint-venture operations, Pertamina exports crude, products and natural gas. It also engages in activities outside the oil and gas industry although these have a much lower profile than previously. It was partly these additional interests that led to Pertamina's poor and much criticized performance in the 1970s and to some curtailing of its independence.

Under Ibnu Sutowo, Pertamina followed a policy of using Indonesia's oil resources to modernize and develop high technology industries. Sutowo conceived the company as being dedicated to the development of the country's oil and gas revenues and as an enterprise central to the development of the overall economy. The benefits to be accrued would filter down to other sectors. For a state oil company to be regarded as a bottomless pit of wealth and patronage is not unknown in other countries in both the developing and developed world. Certainly, it is to the credit of the Indonesian government that firm action was taken before the effect on the economy as a whole had become too disastrous.

Until the reorganization in 1976, Pertamina operated as a fully integrated company and, as the oil industry became the focus of growth for other industrial enterprises, it ran itself as a kind of national development corporation for Indonesia. It became deeply involved in enterprises unrelated to the oil industry, such as the Krakatau steel mill and rice plantations in southern Sumatra. It also, for example, made a substantial entry into the international tanker market in order to integrate its oil operations at an international level. This move was apparently unauthorized and not generally known for some time. Pertamina's entrepreneurial activities and the close personal links between Sutowo and President Suharto circumvented the apparent control of the ministry and led to lack of accountability.

Pertamina had to borrow substantially using relatively short-term loans, mainly from international banks, to implement its ambitious schemes.[8] It was apparently instructed, on direct presidential orders in some cases, to develop some non-oil projects without an adequate budget being allocated to finance them. Loan repayments increased and the company got into severe financial difficulties. It was heavily criticized at the time for borrowing so heavily and committing very large amounts of the country's foreign exchange to projects without conducting any preliminary feasibility studies.

There were valuable achievements by Pertamina and much experience gained; and some of the company's downfall may have been hastened by jealousies within the various governing groups in the country and by hostility from outside the country. However, by the early 1970s, Pertamina had become a state within a state exhibiting considerable extravagance and very poor financial mangement. The company was able to retain most of the revenue from the foreign oil companies and government economists had little influence over its policies or use of funds. Indeed, its investments and payments throughout Indonesia were said to be altering the effect of the government's regional policies.

Pertamina lost its authority to raise funds abroad as a result of the various scandals that came to a head in 1975. Most of the enormous foreign debts, possibly in excess of $10.5 billion, incurred through various unauthorized operations were settled by the government by the end of the 1970s. Subsequently, much closer control than previously began to be exercised over the company's activities. A decree issued in December 1975 confined Pertamina expressly to oil and gas and established new lines of control. Authority now flows vertically to six departmental directors who are responsible to the President Director. The latter, in turn, reports to a Supervisory Board (Board of Commissioners) which exercises real control.[9] In March 1976, Major General Piet Haryono, a military financial administrator, was appointed as President Director. The new role of Pertamina was described by Haryono at the time: 'If ever there was a time in Pertamina's history when Pertamina grew for its own sake without regard to the economic development of the nation as a whole, that time is in the past. Pertamina does not set development objectives – Pertamina responds to those objectives set by the Government. Pertamina does not lead development – it supports it.'[10]

By 1979, much of the non-oil business had been dismantled and the company had largely, although not wholly, reverted to its statutory role as an oil and gas enterprise. Pertamina is still

allowed to involve itself in some outside interests in support of
its oil and gas business but such activities now seem to be kept
within reasonable bounds. Oil and gas revenues are channelled
to central government to finance development plans and there
is a suitable level of auditing.

As a result of the new business climate within Indonesia and
the international oil market, there is currently pressure to
establish a semi-autonomous trading arm to develop trading
skills and market exploration and development expertise overseas. However, this does not, as yet, seem to be in sight.

In the mid-1960s there was considerable controversy over
whether relations with foreign oil companies should take the
form of contracts with the state oil company and remain outside
the legislative prerogative of parliament or whether all relations
with foreign companies should be subject to parliamentary
approval. This was resolved in 1967 with Pertamina acquiring
a special status within the political hierarchy with all oil contracts
being approved by the president, thus bypassing the Ministry of
Mines. This arrangement continues today and, if only on
practical grounds, seems likely to continue. Contracts with a
participating foreign or domestic company are all signed with
Pertamina. The responsibility for overseeing activity under the
contracts rests with the Foreign Contractors Management Body
(BPPKA); although this is actually a part of the Pertamina
organization. The BPPKA reviews budgets and work programmes and the contractors' recommendations for awarding
contracts associated with projects. It plays the determining role
in establishing the commercial viability of any discoveries and
oversees all phases of the contractors' activities.

Pertamina is no longer the self-willed prestige state within a
state that it once was. The Minister of Mines and Energy,
currently I.B. Sudjana, exercises 'day to day' supervisory
authority over Pertamina through Migas. Pertamina also receives
advice from the Board of Commissioners. All major policy
decisions on hydrocarbon investment, production and pricing
appear to be taken by the government primarily in the form of
the Minister of Mines and Energy and the country's president.
However, the National Development Planning Agency
(Bappenas) and key ministers such as the Coordinating Minister
for Industry and Trade (currently Hartarto) play important roles

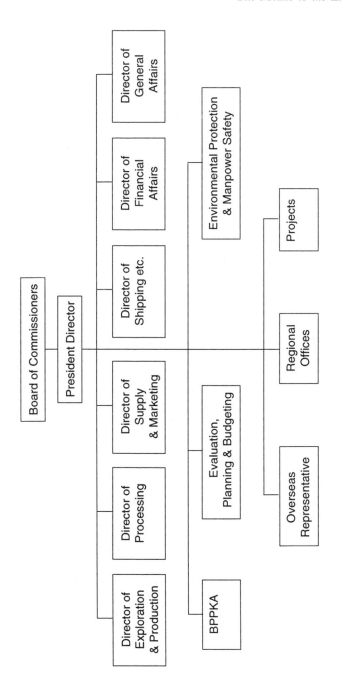

Source: *Oil and Gas Journal*, 16 August, 1993

**Figure 6.2:** Organization of Pertamina

in major policy decisions. The interlocking directorships and chairmen of the various bodies involved in energy matters should allow a reasonable consensus to be developed.

Pertamina remains the main instrument of government policy on hydrocarbons and a major employer with some 47,000 people. It still has considerable freedom of action even though there is more close supervision from outside than in the highly independent days of the 1960s and 1970s. In recent years, Pertamina has been improving its managerial and technical abilities in a planned and determined way. It is now a much more businesslike and practical organization than it has ever been – as indeed it needs to be if it is to optimize Indonesia's hydrocarbon resources. Nonetheless, as long as Indonesia remains basically a military state with a style of government that maintains patronage and close personal ties in business, there is always a danger of Pertamina reverting to its old profligate ways. It is perhaps salutary to note that, although Pertamina has been in existence in one form or another since the earliest days of the Republic, it is still only directly involved in 4 per cent or so of crude oil produced and 3 per cent of gas produced.

Despite Pertamina's continuing grip on the country's oil and gas industry, the government's more open economic policy is already making modest inroads into its domain. This will inevitably increase and may be a process that accelerates in the coming years if overall government ecomomic policy does not go into reverse. Such a process should have a beneficial influence on the emergence of Pertamina as an efficient and dedicated oil and gas business.

In line with the government's privatization policies, Pertamina has licensed private operators for about 300 service stations out of a total of 1,200 and may spin off some more Pertamina owned stations. It has also recently broken its own monopoly to import fuel by licensing an independent power producer to import diesel fuel. In addition, the government issued regulations in 1992 allowing 100 per cent foreign ownership of refineries and petrochemical plants valued in excess of US $50 million. As a result some projects originally conceived as fully owned by Pertamina may eventually materialize as foreign owned. Thus, liberalization of the overall economy is leading to some changes in downstream oil policies and perhaps eventually to a further loss of Pertamina's influence. The changes may well go further but neither mainstream political nor popularist views seem likely to allow a large-scale overt diminition of Pertamina's dominance of the oil and gas sector for many years to come.

## The Relationship with OPEC

In the 1970s, Indonesia was called by some journalists the 'quiet member' of OPEC.[11] This may, in part, have been a reflection of its lack of stridency on the international scene compared with some members. It may also have been because the country was in practice well to the fore in achieving what others were still striving for. Indonesia had full ownership of its oil and gas resources well before the other members of OPEC. In Pertamina and its predecessors it had a very useful instrument for domestic and international activities. Indeed, until the National Iranian Oil Company achieved full control of oil operations in Iran in 1973, Pertamina was the only state company in OPEC that 'owned' all oil and gas resources and also all facilities for production, transport and marketing, including export tankers. Netback pricing was already a feature of the work contracts in 1963. The subsequent introduction of PSCs emphasized the reduced importance to the Indonesian government of royalty and posted price matters, on which other OPEC members expended so much time and effort.

In truth, Indonesia has played an active, although fairly low key role in OPEC since it joined in 1962. Its pioneering of work contracts and PSCs as well as the role of Pertamina have influenced other members. Indonesia's relations with OPEC in its heyday were perhaps best summed up in a luncheon address given by Dr Sadli at the 47th Conference of OPEC member countries in Bali in May 1976. In this address, Dr Sadli indicated that Indonesia would always comply with OPEC decisions for the common interests of the organization as well as the interests of Indonesia itself. He pointed out that Indonesia realized that as an OPEC member country with little oil to export, it does not have a significant influence on OPEC itself, but it was clear that Indonesia greatly benefited from what OPEC achieved. He added that his country was conscious of the importance of

OPEC as a political power. This took place in the days when OPEC was indeed seen as a formidable body, and the reality has of course changed somewhat. Indonesia's policies are now much more set in the context of the markets of South East Asia and must themselves be a considerable influence on the policies of its oil and gas producing neighbours.

The degree of Indonesia's influence on OPEC has, in addition, often been rather greater than relative production strengths would seem to warrant. This has been partially due to the influence of a few individual Indonesians such as Dr Subrotu, the recent OPEC Secretary-General. In general, Indonesia has been supportive of OPEC policies although it has often gone its own way on prices. Indonesia's Law No. 44 bringing all activities under state control and ownership was introduced in 1960. It was not until 1967 that OPEC adopted its 'Declaratory Statement of Oil Policy' in which the member countries would endeavour to pursue an agreed oil policy whereby they would try to enter the oil business themselves or at least place every oil enterprise under control where possible. On oil prices, Indonesia has generally been in the moderate camp, for example in the lead-up to the price increases of 1979.

The country's interests continue to lie in encouraging production restraint by the major Gulf producers to keep oil prices up whilst retaining its own ability to produce to capacity. Generally, over the years Indonesia appears to have complied with the various production quotas and ceilings agreed within OPEC. Certainly since the reimposition of production restraints in 1986, Indonesia has taken care to keep largely within its quota (see Table 6.1). It did increase output to 1.45 mb/d of crude oil in the first half of 1990 after the cessation of Kuwaiti and Iraqi exports but this was with the agreement of OPEC. In most, if not all, years keeping below the ceiling has probably not been too onerous as production levels usually appear to have been set fairly close to Indonesia's apparent production capacity. There is also some flexibility on condensates and natural gas liquids, which are not generally included or are treated ambiguously in OPEC restraints.

At the sixth meeting of OPEC's Ministerial Monitoring Committee in February 1992, Indonesia agreed to continue abiding by the production allocation of 1,374,000 b/d of crude

**Table 6.1**:   Production Quotas for Crude Oil Applied to Indonesia
Compared with Actual Production. Thousand Barrels Per Day

|  | *Quotas* | *Production* |
|---|---|---|
| 1982 | 1,300 | 1,325 |
| 1983 | 1,300 | 1,323 |
| 1984 | 1,189 | 1,227 |
| 1985 | 1,189 | 1,200 |
| December 1986 | 1,190 (Quota Agreement) | 1,267 (1986) |
| October 1988 | 1,190 (Basic Quota) | 1,247 (1987) |
|  | 1,263 (Ceiling) | 1,178 (1988) |
| November 1988 | 1,240 (Quota) |  |
| First Half of 1989 | 1,240 |  |
| Second Half of 1989 | 1,307 | 1,231 (1989) |
| First Half of 1990 | 1,374 |  |
| Second Half of 1990 | 1,374 | 1,281 (1990) |
| 1991 | 1,374 | 1,411 |
| 1992 | 1,374 | 1,347 |
| 1993 | 1,374 | 1,350 |
| 1994 | 1,330 | 1,330 |

Sources: *OPEC Annual Statistical Bulletin, World Oil Report,* December 1994; *Middle East Economic Survey,* various issues; *Petroleum Report of Indonesia,* 1994

oil that was applicable before the Gulf War. Since then the Indonesian Minister for Mines and Energy has repeatedly asked OPEC members producing above their quotas to reduce production in order to boost prices. The OPEC Ministerial Conference held in Bali in November 1994 agreed on a twelve-month roll-over on production quotas, thus extending the Indonesian quota of 1,330 thousand b/d into 1995.

OPEC is useful to a relatively small-scale oil producing country like Indonesia as long as it receives prices that are above the level that would otherwise be obtained and there is some apparent price stability. If the larger producing members of OPEC are unable to deliver on prices, then Indonesia's need for membership must become rather slight.

As a country, Indonesia has managed to build up a broad agricultural and industrial base that, with luck, will continue to steadily reduce the importance of oil to the economy. As an exporter of hydrocarbons, it sells oil and gas largely into the Pacific Rim market which is increasingly writing its own rules.

At the end of the day it may only be nostalgia and the wish to appear on as many world stages as possible that keeps Indonesia in OPEC.

## Notes

1. Only Nigeria has a lower income per head ($290 compared with $570 in 1992). Indonesia has the lowest proved oil reserves other than Qatar and Gabon, the lowest gas reserves other than Libya, Kuwait and Gabon, the lowest crude oil production capacity other than Algeria, Qatar and Gabon. *World Development Report*, 1992; *BP Statistical Review of Energy*, 1993; *OIES Review of Long-Term Energy Supplies*, 1990.
2. Government revenues from oil and gas have grown only modestly from 10 trillion Rp in 1988 to around 13 trillion in 1993. In contrast, non-hydrocarbon domestic revenues have gone up over the same period from 10 trillion Rp to 33 trillion. *Asian Development Outlook*, 1993; *Indonesia: Source Book*, 1993.
3. The government's current privatization programme will include subsidiaries of Pertamin. Pertamina itself will not be privatized but its subsidiaries, especially those fully involved in business activities, can go international. *Asian Energy News*, February 1994.
4. The Directorate General of Power and Energy Development oversees PLN, hydro developments, geothermal and so on. The National Atomic Energy Authority responsible for the nuclear fuel cycle reports directly to the Cabinet.
5. Permigan had as its basis the takeover by a workers' committee of the old BPM Kawenga fields in Central Java. In North Sumatra, Permina took over from a *de facto* company, North Sumatra Oil Industries which had already taken over BPM fields and refineries in North Sumatra. PT Permina was formally established on 10 December, 1957 as a limited liability company with Dr Ibnu Sutowu as its head. Permindo took over NIAM concessions in Central Sumatra and was to become Pertamin. The Tokyo agreement of June 1967 was concluded between Pertamin and Shell. At the time it seemed as if each state company was directly taking over the concessions from the three international companies. Pertamin, between July 1964 and July 1965, took control of, and paid for, the marketing assets of Stanvac, Caltex and Shell. Pertamin was always the most prominent and active of the state companies and in August 1968, Permina and Pertamin were merged as part of a general centralization programme. B.Glassburner et al, *The Economy of Indonesia*, 1971; S.Carlson, *Indonesia's Oil*.
6. Perusahaan Negara Pertambangan Minyak dan Gas Bumi Nasional or National Oil and Gas Company. The merger took place under Law No. 28 of August 1968. O.J. Bee, *The Petroleum Resources of Indonesia*.
7. This was established through Law No. 8 of 1971 (The Petroleum Law) which came into effect on 1 January, 1972. It established a new

corporation, Pertamina, in place of P.N. Pertamina. It also created a Government Council of Commissioners to determine Pertamina's general policy and approve its policies, budget, joint ventures and other transactions. Ibid.

8. In its early years, Pertamina was able to finance its smaller projects from the substantial revenues it was obtaining from the oil companies who had signed PSCs. But as both the scale and number of its commitments increased it had to borrow heavily mainly from international banks to implement its projects. Ibid.

9. Currently (1994) consisting of: I.B. Sudjana (Chairman); Mar'ie Muhammed, Minister of Finance, (Deputy Chairman), the Minister for National Development Planning and Chairman of Bappinas, G. Kartasasmita; the Minister of Research and Technology, B.J. Habibie; Minister/State Secretary, B. Moerdiono.

10. Originally quoted in *Pertamina Today*, 1979.

11. *Far Eastern Economic Review*, 11 Febuary, 1974.

# 7 WITH HOPE INTO THE NEXT CENTURY

## The Challenge

It has been seen that Indonesia possesses substantial resources of oil, gas and coal as well as other natural advantages, including a resourceful and energetic population. It has also had many years of relative political stability with substantial flows of international aid and investment funds from its more industrialized Asian neighbours.

After the oil boom years of the 1970s and early 1980s, the economy has held up remarkably well through the era of low oil prices. Success in diversifying the economy and building up a manufacturing base has been real and substantial growth has been achieved. During the first four years of the 1990s growth in GDP has averaged around 6.5 per cent per annum. However, Indonesia is far from satisfying the aspirations of its very large and young population. It is 10 to 20 years behind Thailand and Malaysia in terms of economic development.

The goal of the Second Twenty-Five Year Development Plan which started in 1994 is to achieve a per capita income of over $3,000 and to enter the ranks of the 'newly industrialized economies'. To achieve this level of income and to fulfil its aim of becoming a major regional economic force, Indonesia will have to go even faster along the development route than it managed at the height of the oil boom. For example, just to reach by the year 2010 the average per capita income enjoyed by Malaysia at present, would require a quadrupling of income levels and the economy to grow at an average of over 9 per cent per annum.[1] Such growth will necessitate the successful fulfilment of many conditions. Of these, a continuation of political stability together with the broadening and expansion of the manufacturing sector into a major source of exports and a competitive supplier for the home market are probably the most important. Inextricably bound up with both political stability and the building up of the economy is the need to expand the development of the country's oil and gas resources.

In any country as large and diverse as Indonesia, there is always the possibility of political instability, internal strife and even disintegration as a unified state. With Indonesia's special problems and the over-concentration of development on Java, any future government of whatever complexion will find it difficult to maintain the relative political and social stability of the past 27 years. This will be particularly so because of the earlier success in smoothing over and localizing problems. President Suharto has another four years in office, at the end of which he will be 77 years old. The present governmental and business arrangements are likely to survive as long as he remains in power. They may even be continued after he has gone, through the medium of well-groomed successors drawn from the armed forces.

Much will depend on the armed forces (ABRI), who are seen by many in the business community and elsewhere as the continuing guarantors of stability. The transition from the old generation of military leaders to the new generation without a background in the freedom struggle is now almost complete. Whether Suharto stands down before or at the end of his present term of office or even continues for another term, his influence on a replacement will be strong. The transition could be smooth leading to a much more democratic country as occurred in Spain after the death of General Franco. On the other hand there is enormous potential for conflict between and often within the different factions in the country. These include the armed forces,[2] the president's family and associates, the business community, Muslim fundamentalism and, not least, the variety of different population groupings of this enormous country. The next few years of Suharto's presidency seem likely to be critical. He has to balance the demands of all these groups whilst attracting the investment and skills needed to keep the economy, at the very least, ahead of the growth in population.

The rise to prominence in the 1993 Cabinet reshuffle of B.J. Habibie and the dismissal of three economic technocrat ministers[3] set alarm bells ringing over the future direction of the economy. Habibie has always been a strong and plausible advocate of big industrial projects – usually with a strongly nationalistic flavour, such as aircraft manufacturing, ship building, nuclear power and petrochemical plants. Although supporting such industries in the past led to great difficulties, it may be argued that time has moved on and there is now a sounder basis for such projects. In any case, controlling inflation, keeping a balanced budget and limiting offshore borrowing are now so firmly a part of policy that the dangers of investment in such projects getting out of hand are limited. Nonetheless, these industries create few new jobs and usually in fields in which Indonesia finds it difficult to compete internationally. Thus, they require protective measures which in themselves distort and adversely affect the overall economy. The country's relative advantages in international competition lie with its cheap, abundant labour and its agricultural, mineral and hydrocarbon resources.

It is perhaps a truism that the government needs to step up its efforts to attract direct foreign investment into sound projects. There are many other countries in the area all competing for such funds, not least China and India, where the terms available are generally better. In addition, Indonesia cannot limit itself to depending on foreign capital given the size of its economy and its aspirations. It must also encourage the emergence of robust local enterprises. As a part of this, the need to streamline the bureaucracy has long been recognized.[4] Certainly, since the liberalization of the financial market in 1988, the government has taken steps towards easing restrictions. The market liberalization package announced in June 1993 has made it a little more difficult for the government to intervene in economic activity than before and given some encouragement to domestic and international investors. However, as long as the existing administrative structure serves as a foundation for the party in power and the president's family and associates and the armed forces continue to play such a major business role, sound investment and growth will be hampered.

It is impossible and perhaps foolish to even try to predict whether the late 1990s will see a transition to a less concentrated and firm form of government. Or indeed whether this would lead to economic and social chaos or to a more open, democratic and successful climate for the economy and the country as a whole. Success with the economy is essential to keep the many potential destabilizing elements at bay. One has to hope that the Indonesian genius for compromise and the ability to placate can continue to work its magic.

In developing and diversifying the economy away from its former reliance on oil, a significant measure of success has already been achieved. Many economic distortions remain, particular in the domestic economy, which remains blighted by public and private monopolies enjoying a high level of protection. However, the rules on foreign investment have been relaxed and there are moves towards greater privatization and the number of export orientated manufacturing industries has increased considerably. Nonetheless, the oil and gas industry still provides around 30 per cent of export earnings and is the single largest source of government revenues. These earnings from oil and gas will continue to be vital, well into the next century, if economic growth is to be sustained and broadened. Unfortunately, as discussed in the earlier chapters, there is a very real danger that domestic oil demand could within a few years outstrip production and make the continuation of net exports of oil impossible.

## The Future of Energy Demand and Supply

Over and above the pressures from the inexorable rise in population, the actual level of energy demand will depend strongly on the pace and pattern of economic growth and on the potential for improving energy intensity. However, the drive towards industrialization and increasing urbanization will make the achievement of significant improvements in the overall intensity of energy use very difficult.

Even in conjunction with modest economic growth, it is likely that demand for commercial energy will at least have doubled by the year 2010. An extra 1.5 mboe/d or so of energy would need to be found for domestic consumption alone. At the same time substantial volumes of energy will be needed as replacement for the depleted oil, gas and coal fields.

Some of the additional energy required will come from increased capacity of renewable resources, mainly hydro and geothermal as well as from the new and upgraded coal facilities. Indeed, coal in particular is already on course to becoming a major source of fuel for power generation and foreign exchange earnings. However, it seems unlikely in the light of present plans and the potential scope, that much more than 25–30 mt (300–400,000 boe/d) of additional coal could be utilized in domestic markets over the next 17 years or so. An additional 5 to 10 GW

(100–200,000 boe/d) of hydro and geothermal power could perhaps be made available but it is clear that the bulk of incremental domestic demand for energy will have to be met by oil and, increasingly, by gas. This, at best, would probably mean a demand for oil for use in domestic markets alone of at least 1.4 mb/d by the end of the first decade of the next century. This is close to the entire amount of oil currently being produced; out of which 0.8 mb/d is currently exported. For economic growth to be sustained at somewhat above current levels through to the year 2010, domestic demand for oil will have to grow by at least 5 per cent per annum even with improvements in overall energy intensity. This would mean a demand of 1.9 mb/d, which is well above current oil production of 1.7 mb/d (see Appendix 10 for details).

The actual rate at which domestic oil demand will grow in future from its present level of around 800,000 b/d is, of course, highly uncertain. Some outside projections[5] take an optimistic view of the progress of substitution and expect only very modest increases in oil demand, averaging 10,000 b/d or less per annum. This may be unrealistic. Growth in oil demand, encouraged by a cheap oil policy, has averaged around 7 per cent per annum in the recent past. Although subsidies on domestic fuels have now largely been removed, growing affluence will be reflected in increased intensity of oil use in households. In addition, the potential in an expanding economy for restricting growth in vehicle use, the fastest growing source of oil demand, is very limited.

The present product imbalance and middle distillate deficit is being addressed through new refinery facilities although some are currently in abeyance. It is to be hoped that this will not result in the new export refineries having to import substantial quantities of crude oil to meet customers' pattern of product demand.

Creating the right fiscal and business climate for the wider use of Liquefied Petroleum Gas (LPG) in domestic markets would also be of help in improving the overall energy economy. The bulk of LPG is currently being shipped abroad and makes a very useful contribution to export earnings. It seems likely that, with the gas projects currently planned and with increased supplies from new liquefied natural gas facilities, substantial additional supplies of LPG will be available through the 1990s. The move to full parity with international prices for domestic kerosene and the effect of rising incomes should help to encourage the use of LPG in households across the income ranges. The continued rapid electrification of the country will also have a beneficial effect on domestic oil use as most new capacity is likely to be gas or coal fired.

Despite the range of other influences, the major contribution to moderating oil demand will, it seems likely, have to come from greater use of natural gas. Substantially increased gas penetration is already underway as a result of the development of gas fields for direct domestic use. This is affecting future demand for oil for power generation and will increasingly affect the pattern of industrial energy use as more such projects are developed. Together with technologically led efficiency improvements, average annual growth in oil demand could perhaps be reduced to as little as 4 per cent or so in future. Even if one then takes another seemingly optimistic view, that crude oil and natural gas liquids production can be maintained at current levels into the next century, the volume of oil available for export would inevitably fall.[6] Towards the end of the next decade there would be scarcely any oil available for export.

The maintenance of an adequate level of liquid fuels production to enable oil exports to continue contributing to the economy for as long as possible, even as domestic demand for oil increases, is clearly a major challenge.[7] A much greater use of natural gas and coal in place of oil in domestic markets is an approach which must go hand in hand with trying to increase oil production capacity.

## Increasing Oil Production

Just to keep oil production at around recent levels will require a continuing major effort; between 400 and 500 mb would need to be proved up each year. This has not been achieved in recent years and improvements in the maturing oil provinces of Indonesia under increasingly difficult conditions will not be easy. As indicated earlier, the maintenance of production at current levels will not be enough if exports are to be maintained. Even with substantial penetration of gas and coal into domestic markets, production of crude and natural gas liquids would probably need to be increased to over 2 mb/d and sustained well into the next century to provide adequate leeway. This would require a discovery rate of over 1 billion barrels per annum.

There is some indication that the oil resources needed to support increased production levels may well be present in the archipelago. Most fields currently producing are small and not very productive and the overwhelming bulk of crude production still comes from four main fields. Past exploration has tended to be concentrated mainly in these known areas and many potential oil-bearing areas have yet to be explored adequately. A much greater degree of activity is needed in the offshore and remote areas as well as the further application of advanced recovery methods to mature fields. This is, of course, well recognized by the government and Pertamina.

Current oil reserves were largely built up during two periods of intensive exploration, in the 1940s and the 1960s. Production declined through the 1980s and there was a particularly low level of exploration activity in the mid-1980s. Its impact is still being felt. Another problem is that new discoveries have tended to be of heavier and less valuable crudes than the typical Indonesian high quality, low sulphur, medium gravity crudes such as Minas. Nonetheless, after declining through most of the 1980s, production of crude oil and natural gas liquids has been increasing in recent years. Production is now very close to its 1978 peak.

Although the third major phase of oil exploration in modern Indonesia is currently underway, exploration results have not been particularly good. Contract signings in the first year of this decade were at or near record levels, partly reflecting changes in pricing policy and more flexible contract terms. Signings have in subsequent years fallen drastically and there have been a number of relinquishments, mainly as a result of disappointment over terms and the attractions of activity in other countries. This does not augur well for production levels during the rest of the 1990s and beyond. A very slight counter to this is that there may be substantial additional volumes of natural gas liquids becoming available through the 1990s. This should be as a result of the planned expansion of gas production and liquefied natural gas facilities.

Increased oilfield activity that hopefully leads to increased production will continue to hinge on attracting investment and technology from foreign oil companies. It is likely that this will need to be much greater than in the past. Pertamina has been greatly improved from its profligate days of the 1970s; however, it cannot hope by itself to find more than a fraction of the financial, technical and managerial resources needed to develop Indonesia's hydrocarbon resources. There may need to be a loosening of its present all-embracing role in the oil and gas sector.

Apart from basic business confidence derived from economic and political stability, it is the attractiveness of the terms offered to foreign companies that will decide how much activity takes place. There will be many investment opportunities in energy projects available in various countries over the next decade or so. The choice of where to invest for those international companies with extensive expertise and available funds is very wide.

Indonesia introduced the once revolutionary concept of production-sharing arrangements for oil and gas development. These arrangements were seen as a way of attracting foreign oil companies to provide the funds and expertise to develop the industry whilst still maintaining full control of its national resources. The PSC remains the country's preeminent legal form for the exploration and production of oil and gas, although it has seen several major changes since it was first used in the mid-1960s. It was certainly a useful device for the situation pertaining in the 1960s, but it is not clear whether it has been the best vehicle to attract exploration and development investment. Perhaps some other contractual form, such as major joint ventures giving real equity rights, might have built up reserves in Eastern Indonesia more quickly and substantially.

The government has always sought to negotiate contracts that satisfy its political imperative of maintaining, and being seen to assert, its sovereign rights over oil and gas. The reality of attracting investment and expertise from foreign companies has necessitated a degree of pragmatism and innovation on terms. In recent years, the government and Pertamina have shown themselves to be increasingly flexible. There have been four packages of incentives since 1988 and there are now also a variety of contractual arrangements possible in addition to the PSC. These new arrangements have been mainly directed at encouraging exploration and development in marginal areas. However, they do not appear to have been very successful in attracting investment by major international companies in new areas.

Past policies seem to have led to a large number of deals of relatively small scope with new and often minor players. This would appear to spread the technical and administrative effort rather thinly. What may be needed is a more positive and consistent effort to attract major players. Certainly, substantial and sustained investment and technical expertise will be needed to boost production significantly. The question is whether the government is willing and confident enough to go further down the road of providing the more flexible and attractive terms. A test case may well prove to be the terms finally agreed for the development of Natuna gas.

Although oil will continue to play a major role, the country's development will increasingly rest on other foundations. Not least of these will be the further and broader development of natural gas.

## Natural Gas Goes Ahead

In the past Indonesia has been very successful in developing its gas resources for export. It has been in the right place at the right time. The country is ideally placed geographically to supply the Japanese need for a clean fuel and to supply the energy requirements of the new expanding industries of South East Asia. It has also managed to get its gas into the international market-place in substantial volumes well ahead of other suppliers and, thus, to build up long-term relationships with the markets.

Increasing exports of natural gas have, for many years, been successfully helping to counter falling exports of oil. From producing barely 1 bcm per annum of natural gas in the early 1970s, Indonesia is now producing well over 50 bcm and is the world's largest exporter of liquefied natural gas.

There is a deal of uncertainty on the size of the resource base for gas. Nonetheless, the potential seems to be substantial and further exploration and development should continue to enhance reserves considerably. This is particularly so as additional gas reserves from smaller fields are beginning to be seen as a target in their own right with a ready and valuable market, rather than as a mere by-product of oil exploration.

The successful development of the Natuna gas field would give Indonesia the basis for sustaining its present gas exports well into the next century. In addition, the start of major activity at Natuna may well provide just the confidence in the commercial future of the country's gas industry that could stimulate massive gas activity throughout the archipelago. If smaller discoveries in known areas can also be successfully exploited, then exports could be substantially increased in volume.

The extent of the long-term potential for additional gas exports into the Asian market is a major uncertainty in the future of Indonesian gas exports and there is a great deal of jockeying for commercial position amongst suppliers. Considerable competition is developing for Indonesian gas exports from other suppliers in the Pacific Basin and elsewhere. Much depends on the continuation of the general economic dynamism of the region and on the growing preference for gas by energy consumers. Nonetheless, even under less buoyant conditions, the competitive position for an experienced supplier such as Indonesia must be favourable. The ongoing long-term contracts, the sound commercial relationships built up over many years and the possession of established plant, will all help as a basis for expanding export volumes.

In the past, priority was given to gas for export but there is growing emphasis on the need to use gas to substitute for oil in domestic markets. Investment in new gas facilities, either for export or domestic use, is highly capital intensive. It generally requires a much longer-term outlook and stronger bonds of mutual confidence between producers and purchasers than for oil development. This is, no doubt, well understood by the Indonesian government but perhaps more needs to be done to provide attractive and market indexed returns on developments specifically for domestic use.

As with oil, many known gas reserves are remote and the vast and underexplored regions of eastern Indonesia may also contain sizeable gas reserves. The circumstances in these regions, with small populations and modest infrastructure, may favour a more imaginative approach to development, such as the conversion of the gas to liquids. This would enable a substantial local market to be available as well as reduced shipping costs for moving the gas elsewhere in the country. Certainly, in looking at the future development of Indonesia's gas resources, expensive additions to LNG capacity must be considered in the light of cheaper alternatives based on domestic pipelines. The maintenance of an optimum balance between investing for additional gas exports and building the infrastructure for increased domestic use will be a major challenge.

If a clear, reliable and flexible policy for attracting the substantial long-term investment that is always needed for gas projects can be maintained, natural gas should be able eventually to replace oil as Indonesia's main source of domestic energy. There seems little reason, other than a lack of business confidence, why gas sales should not also continue to expand as a major source of export earnings.

## A Bright Future?

The country has come a long way since the strident and prickly nationalism of the 1960s and 1970s. There is now a much higher level of technical and administrative ability and much greater self confidence. This is combined with growing pragmatism and with a more realistic anticipation of market conditions and a less confrontational approach to outside interests. Indonesia has been remarkably successful in the past in maintaining political stability and economic growth through major setbacks and difficulties. The achievements in reducing poverty and increasing the general well-being of the population as a whole have been substantial despite nepotism, elitism and other practices. The country's energy resources, particularly oil and gas, have played a major part in this and could continue to do so. The successful exploitation of oil and gas resources will remain vital to the future economic success and political stability of Indonesia. In turn, the ability to attract the capital and skills needed to develop energy resources rests on the international business perception of Indonesia as a stable country with a sound and expanding economy. The challenge is to build on past successes and develop more rapidly the dynamic and balanced energy economy which the country needs for self sustained economic development.

With continued enterprise and good fortune there is a very bright future in store for Indonesia and its many inhabitants. The optimization of its energy resources, particularly of oil and gas, is a fundamental prerequisite.

## Notes

1.  Government ministers have been reported as indicating that 7 per cent per annum is the maximum growth the country can achieve without overheating the economy. *Financial Times*, 13 May, 1993.
2.  The transfer from the older generation of military men to a new generation without the direct experience of the struggle for freedom is likely to increase the strains on unity within the armed forces, which in any case were never completely homogenous.
3.  R. Prawiro, J.B. Sumarlin and A. Mooy. Replaced by Saleh Afiff, M. Muhammad and Sudrajat Djiwandono as Coordination Minister for the economy and finance, Finance Minister and Central Bank Governor respectively.
4.  President Suharto addressed the issue in a speech to Parliament in August 1993. He stated 'we shall loosen restrictions and reform the bureaucracy, as well as reduce and eliminate subsidies and protective measures in order to improve the competitive strength of private corporations.' M. Hayashida, *The Three Mini-Dragons*.
5.  M. Imran and P. Barnes, *Energy Demand in Developing Countries*.
6.  1.5 mb/d domestic demand by 2010 compared with oil production of 1.6 mb/d.
7.  A projection of Indonesian crude and condensate production from Petroleum Argus and East–West Centre (21 March, 1994) put production at 1.4 mb/d in 1995 and at 1.0 mb/d in 2000, of which 0.55 mb/d is still Minas and Duri crudes.

# APPENDIX 1
## Map of Indonesia

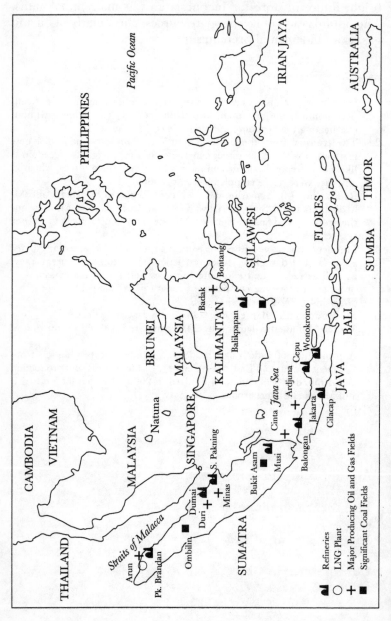

# APPENDIX 2
## Basic Demographic, Economic and Political Data

**Area:** 1.905 million sq. km.

**Capital:** Jakarta

**Population:** 191 million (mid 1992)

**Urban Population as Per Cent of Total:** 31 per cent (1990)

**Projected Growth in Population:** 1.6 per cent average annual increase (1995–2000)

**Currency:** Rupiah (Rp)

**Inflation:** 9.8 per cent (1993/1992)

**Market Exchange Rate:** 2,100–2,200 Rp per $ (1993)

**GDP:** 127,192 million US $ (1992)

**GDP Per Capita:** 682 US $ (1992)

**Official Development Assistance:** 1,724 million US $ (1990) (1.6 per cent of 1990 GDP)

**Annual Exports (f.o.b)** 3.6 billion US $ (1993)

**Annual Imports (c.i.f)** 28.1 billion US $ (1993)

**President of Indonesia:** Suharto

**Vice President of Indonesia:** Try Sutrisno

**Commander in Chief of the Armed Forces (ABRI)**
Feisal Tanjung

**Chairman of National Development Planning Agency (Bappenas):**   Ginandjar Kartasasmita

**Minister of Mines and Energy:**   I.B Sudjana

**State Minister of Research and Technology, Chairman of the Agency for the Assessment and Application of Technology (BPPT):**   B.J. Habibie

**OPEC Governor:**   Suyitno Patmosukismo

**President Director of Pertamina:**   Faisal Abda'oe

**President Director of PGN:**   H. Abdul Qoyum Tjandranegara

**Director General of Migas:**   Suyitno Patmosukismo

**Chairman of Bakoren:**   I.B Sudjana

## APPENDIX 3
### Chronology of the Indonesian Oil and Gas Industry 1885–1994

| | |
|---|---|
| **1885** | First commercial oil struck at Telaga Tungal in East Sumatra (15.6) |
| **1890** | Refinery constructed at Wonokrono Royal Dutch formed and takes over concession in East Java (10.6) |
| **1892** | Shell Transport and Trading discovers oil in East Kalimantan and constructs a refinery at Balikpapan |
| **1899** | East Indies Oil Mining Act passed |
| **1906** | All oil companies are integrated into Royal Dutch or obliged to deliver crude oil to this company |
| **1907** | Royal Dutch merges with Shell Transport and Trading |
| **1912** | Stanvac begins operations in the country |
| **1930** | Socal forms a subsidiary in the country |
| **1936** | Socal merges with Texaco to form Caltex Pacific and begins exploration |
| **1941** | Duri field discovered |
| **1942** | Japanese troops land at Tarakan. Installations set on fire |
| **1944** | Discovery well of Minas field (location readied in late 1941 by Caltex) |
| **1945** | Japanese surrender |
| | Indonesian independence declared (17.8) |
| **1949** | Independence achieved (December) |
| **1951** | Crude oil production regains prewar levels at 173,000 b/d |
| **1952** | Production begins at Minas field |
| **1954** | Oil agreements are concluded with Stanvac, Shell and Caltex on a profit sharing basis (50/50 basis) |

**1957**    Ibnu Sutowo appointed to establish a limited liability company to rehabilitate the oil industry (15.10) Permina is formed for the rehabilitation of the oil industry and the export of oil

**1960**    Law No. 44 on Petroleum and Gas Mining is enacted (26.10) revoking concession rights of foreign oil companies. Pertamina formed

**1962**    Agreement signed between Permina and Shell for the purchase of Shell's assets in Central and East Java

Indonesia joins OPEC (4.6)

**1963**    Contracts of work signed between the state-owned oil companies and foreign oil companies (1.4)

**1964**    All domestic marketing assets of Shell, Stanvac and Caltex begin to be transferred to Pertamina

**1965**    Agreement signed on the transfer of all Shell's assets in Indonesia

Attempted coup by Communist Party (October)

Decree granting President of Indonesia absolute powers

**1966**    Production-sharing agreement signed between Permina and various small US independent companies

Focus of exploration shifts to offshore areas

President Sukarno removed from office

First offshore production-sharing agreement signed with IIAPCO

**1967**    Ibnu Sutowo appointed Minister of Mines and of Oil and Gas and President Director of Permina

Bureau of Oil and Gas severed from Ministry of Mines and placed directly under the Cabinet

**1968**    General Suharto elected President

Government Regulation No. 27 on the establishment of P.N. Pertamina (7.4.) and Permina and Pertamin merged into single national oil company Pertamina

**1969** Indonesia and Malaysia sign the Continental Shelf Agreement

**1970** Offshore commercial oil production starts in the Cinta and Arzuna fields in North West Java

Secondary recovery programme initiated in Minas field

Heavy attacks on Pertamina over corruption and mismanagement

Thirty production-sharing agreements concluded between Pertamina and foreign oil companies by the end of the year

**1971** Export price of Minas crude raised to $2.60 per barrel (1.10)

Gas discovered at Arun by Mobil

**1972** New corporation, P.T. Pertamina established in place of P.N. Pertamina and conditions established for the entry of Pertamina into fields and activities beyond the oil and gas sector (1.1)

Oil and gas discovered in the Badak field by Roy M. Huffington

**1973** Average price of Minas crude in last quarter $6.16 per barrel

First sales contracts signed for LNG exports (late 1973)

**1974** Virtually all offshore areas contracted out

New profit sharing formula instituted (60/40 on base barrel portion and 85/15 on rest)

Minas crude price reaches $12.60 per barrel in July

**1975** Financial crisis in Pertamina

Pertamina reorganized and non-oil related activities transferred to other government departments and agencies

Further modifications putting profit-sharing formula on to a sliding scale

**1976**   Renegotiation of contracts with companies operating under Contract of Work agreements (Caltex and Stanvac)

Two-tier production-sharing agreement with various allowances etc. related to reserves and production levels introduced

**1977**   First gas exports from Badak and Arun

Crude exports reach peak of 1.3 mb/d

Crude production reaches peak of 1.69 mb/d

**1978**   US IRS declares that payments made by US companies to Indonesia under the terms of the production-sharing agreements are eligible for foreign tax credit in the USA

**1979**   'Cash for oil' agreement with Japanese National Oil Company

**1980**   Indonesia displaces Algeria as world's largest LNG exporter

**1981**   Price of Minas crude reaches peak of $35.00 per barrel (1.1)

**1983**   New oil exploration peaks

**1986**   ASEAN oil trade agreement signed

Abandonment of Government Schedule of Prices as a pricing mechanism for crude oil exports

**1987**   Massive steam flood EOR project introduced by Caltex in the Duri field

**1988**   Oil Minister announces that Indonesia plans to stop exporting crude and will only export products

Subroto becomes Secretary-General of OPEC (July)

New and extension production-sharing contracts

Introduction of variable production-sharing contracts between Pertamina and foreign contractors (31.8)

**1989**   Partial deregulation of foreign exchange dealing

New incentives for production-sharing contracts (22.2)

Agreement between Australia and Indonesia on the establishment of a binational authority to supervise exploration in the Timor Gap

Revision of official oil pricing policy involving the replacement of the GSP with a market related pricing formula (1.4)

Abandonment of official crude oil prices as a basis for index linking of gas contracts and tax liability

Replacement by a pricing formula based on spot prices from a basket of traded crudes

**1990**    Development plans announced for Natuna gas field

Official price of Minas raised from $14.81 in July 1990 to an all-time high of $35.29 in October 1991

**1991**    Gas exports at record level of 385 cargoes and 22 mt

Record 22 production-sharing contracts signed

**1992**    Ruling Golkar Party reelected (9.6)

Third incentives package for upstream contractors

**1993**    Reelection of President Suharto for sixth term (March)

Remaining subsidies on domestic fuel start to be phased out

Conversion of last Contract of Work

**1994**    Introduction of fourth package of incentives allied to PSCs (January)

Asia Pacific Economic Cooperation (Apec) summit held in Jakarta (December)

Subroto relinquishes position as Secretary-General of OPEC (June)

# APPENDIX 4
## Historical Oil Production. Crude and Natural Gas Liquids. Thousand Barrels Per Day

| | |
|---|---|
| 1900 | 6 |
| 1910 | 30 |
| 1920 | 48 |
| 1930 | 114 |
| 1940 | 169 |
| 1950 | 133 |
| 1960 | 419 |
| 1970 | 854 |
| 1971 | 892 |
| 1972 | 1,681 |
| 1973 | 1,338 |
| 1974 | 1,374 |
| 1975 | 1,306 |
| 1976 | 1,504 |
| 1977 | 1,686 |
| 1978 | 1,635 |
| 1979 | 1,591 |
| 1980 | 1,576 |
| 1981 | 1,680 |
| 1982 | 1,415 |
| 1983 | 1,420 |
| 1984 | 1,505 |
| 1985 | 1,340 |
| 1986 | 1,430 |
| 1987 | 1,420 |
| 1988 | 1,375 |
| 1989 | 1,480 |
| 1990 | 1,540 |
| 1991 | 1,670 |
| 1992 | 1,580 |
| 1993 | 1,530 |
| 1994 | 1,510 (provisional) |

Sources:  *Twentieth Century Petroleum Statistics, BP Statistical Review of World Energy*; author's estimates

# APPENDIX 5
## Historical Natural Gas Production (Net Marketed).
## Billion Standard Cubic Metres

| | |
|---|---|
| 1970 | 1 |
| 1971 | 1 |
| 1972 | 1 |
| 1973 | 1 |
| 1974 | 1 |
| 1975 | 2 |
| 1976 | 2 |
| 1977 | 6 |
| 1978 | 11 |
| 1979 | 16 |
| 1980 | 19 |
| 1981 | 19 |
| 1982 | 19 |
| 1983 | 22 |
| 1984 | 33 |
| 1985 | 34 |
| 1986 | 35 |
| 1987 | 37 |
| 1988 | 39 |
| 1989 | 43 |
| 1990 | 48 |
| 1991 | 51 |
| 1992 | 54 |
| 1993 | 56 |
| 1994 | 56 (provisional) |

Sources:  *OPEC Annual Statistical Bulletin*; *Cedigaz News Report*; *Oil and Energy Trends*; author's estimates

## APPENDIX 6
**Historical Domestic Oil Consumption. Thousand Barrels Per Day**

| | |
|---|---|
| 1970 | 111 |
| 1971 | 123 |
| 1972 | 141 |
| 1973 | 163 |
| 1974 | 189 |
| 1975 | 220 |
| 1976 | 238 |
| 1977 | 269 |
| 1978 | 306 |
| 1979 | 346 |
| 1980 | 410 |
| 1981 | 450 |
| 1982 | 465 |
| 1983 | 450 |
| 1984 | 475 |
| 1985 | 460 |
| 1986 | 465 |
| 1987 | 500 |
| 1988 | 525 |
| 1989 | 560 |
| 1990 | 645 |
| 1991 | 675 |
| 1992 | 730 |
| 1993 | 790 |
| 1994 | 840 (provisional) |

Sources:  *BP Statistical Review of World Energy*; *Petroleum Report of Indonesia*; S. Arief, *Financial Analysis of the Indonesian Petroleum Industry*; author's estimates

# APPENDIX 7
## Historical Coal Production. Million Metric Tonnes

| | |
|---|---|
| 1980 | 0.3 |
| 1981 | 0.3 |
| 1982 | 0.4 |
| 1983 | 0.5 |
| 1984 | 1.1 |
| 1985 | 1.5 |
| 1986 | 1.7 |
| 1987 | 3.1 |
| 1988 | 4.5 |
| 1989 | 8.7 |
| 1990 | 10.8 |
| 1991 | 14.5 |
| 1992 | 23.4 |
| 1993 | 26.4 |
| 1994 | 35.0 (provisional) |

Sources: *Oil and Energy Trends*; *UN Energy Statistics Yearbook*; *Indonesia: Source Book*

# APPENDIX 8
## Crude Oil Prices. $ Per Barrel

| | *1990* | *1991* | *1992* | *1993* | *1994* |
|---|---|---|---|---|---|
| Minas (34° API) | 16.30 | 18.01 | 18.20 | 18.67 | 15.76 |
| Duri (20° API) | 14.37 | 15.06 | 14.51 | 16.70 | 12.97 |
| Cinta (28° API) | 15.85 | 17.68 | 17.68 | 18.03 | 15.06 |
| Handil (32° API) | 16.24 | 18.05 | 18.25 | 18.54 | 15.60 |
| Walio (33° API) | 16.12 | 17.81 | 18.00 | 18.47 | 15.56 |
| Ardjuna (37° API) | 16.46 | 19.29 | 18.83 | 18.99 | 15.99 |
| Attaka (41° API) | 17.13 | 18.95 | 19.73 | 19.67 | 16.53 |

'Indonesian Crude Price' in May of Each Year

Source: *International Crude Oil and Product Prices*, July 1994

## APPENDIX 9
**Projected Oil Production Profiles to 2010.**
**Million Barrels Per Day**

|  | Production from Existing Fields | Discoveries /EOR | NGLs | Total |
|---|---|---|---|---|
| **1   High Discovery*** | | | | |
| 1993 | 1.3 | - | 0.2 | 1.5 |
| 1995 | 1.4 | 0.1 | 0.2 | 1.7 |
| 2000 | 1.3 | 0.6 | 0.3 | 2.2 |
| 2005 | 1.1 | 1.3 | 0.3 | 2.7 |
| 2010 | 0.8 | 1.8 | 0.4 | 3.0 |
| **2   Medium Discovery**** | | | | |
| 1995 | 1.3 | Neg. | 0.2 | 1.5 |
| 2000 | 1.0 | 0.2 | 0.2 | 1.4 |
| 2005 | 0.5 | 0.5 | 0.3 | 1.3 |
| 2010 | 0.2 | 0.7 | 0.3 | 1.2 |

\* 1.2 billion barrels per annum (proven reserves 11.2 billion)
\*\* 0.4 billion barrels per annum (proven reserves 6.2 billion)

Source: Author's own projections

# APPENDIX 10
## Projected Demand for Commercial Energy to 2010.
## Thousand Barrels Oil Equivalent Per Day

|  | *1991* | *2010* |
|---|---|---|
| *Primary Energy* | | |
| Oil | 757 | 1,536 |
| Natural Gas | 386 | 656 |
| Coal | 90 | 369 |
| Hydro etc. | 58 | 191 |
| Total | 1,291 | 2,752 |
| *Energy Demand by Markets* | | |
| Transport | 263 | 760 |
| Industry | 305 | 713 |
| Residential and Services | 191 | 416 |
| Total Direct | 759 | 1,889 |
| Electricity Generation | 243 | 662 |
| *Oil Demand by Markets* | | |
| Transport | 263 | 760 |
| Industry | 140 | 238 |
| Residential and Services | 156 | 232 |
| Electricity Generation | 101 | 91 |
| Others | 94 | 215 |
| Total | 754 | 1,536 |

Based on, among other assumptions:
   GDP growth of 6 per cent average annual increase
   Crude oil prices at $15 to $20 per barrel

Source: Author's own projections

# BIBLIOGRAPHY

## Journals, Periodicals, Annuals & Encyclopedias

*Asia Energy News*
*Asian Development Outlook*
*Asian Energy Review*
*BP Review of World Gas*
*BP Statistical Review of World Energy*
*Cedigaz News Report*
*Coal Information*
*The Economist*
*Energy Compass*
*Energy Economics*
*Energy Policy*
*Far Eastern Economic Review*
*Financial Times*
*FT International Gas Report*
*Gas Matters*
*Green Energy Matters*
*Indonesia Quarterly*
*Indonesian Development Quarterly*
*International Crude Oil and Product Prices*
*International Financial Statistics*
*International Petroleum Encyclopedia*
*International Water Power and Dam Construction*
*Middle East Economic Survey*
*Oil and Energy Trends*
*Oil and Gas Journal*
*OPEC Annual Statistical Bulletin*
*OPEC Bulletin*
*Petroleum Intelligence Weekly*
*The Petroleum Quarterly*
*Petroleum Report of Indonesia (US Embassy, Jakarta annually)*
*Twentieth Century Petroleum Statistics*
*Weekly Petroleum Argus*
*World Development Report*
*World Gas Intelligence*
*World Oil*

# Books

Arief, S. (1976), *The Indonesian Petroleum Industry: A Study of Resource Management in a Developing Country*, Jakarta: Sritua Aref Associates.

— (1977), *Financial Analysis of the Indonesian Petroleum Industry*, Jakarta: Sritua Aref Associates.

Barnes, P. (1990), *The OIES Review of Long-Term Energy Supplies*, Oxford Institute for Energy Studies.

Barnes, P. and Y. Nagata, (1983), 'Energy: The Key to Indonesia's Future', unpublished.

Barrows, G. (1993), *Indonesia's Oil and Gas Terms – Latest Status and Trends in Production Sharing, 1966 to 1993*, Presentation to the Institute for International Research (28 April, 1993, Houston), New York: Barrows Company Inc.

Bee, O.J. (1982), *The Petroleum Resources of Indonesia*, Malaysia: Oxford University Press.

Booth, A. (ed.) (1992), *The Oil Boom and After: Indonesian Economic Policy and Performance in the Soeharto Era*, Singapore: Oxford University Press.

Brown, G. (1990), *OPEC and the World Energy Market: A Comprehensive Reference Guide*, London: Longman.

Carlson, S. (1977), *Indonesia's Oil*, Colorado: Westview Press.

Cornot-Gandolphe, S. (1991), *World LNG Trade: A New Growth Phase*, Cedigaz.

Glassburner, B. et al (1971), *The Economy of Indonesia*, Ithaca & London: Cornell University Press.

Hayashida, M. (1994), *The Three Mini-Dragons: Economic Development in Thailand, Malaysia and Indonesia*, Tokyo: Institute for International Policy Studies.

Imran, M. and P. Barnes, (1990), *Energy Demand in the Developing Countries: Prospects for the Future*, World Bank Staff Commodity Working Paper, No. 23, Washington: World Bank.

*Indonesia: Source Book*; see National Development Information Office

Khong, C.O. (1986), *The Politics of Oil in Indonesia: Foreign Company–Host Government Relations*, Cambridge: Cambridge University Press.

Klapp, M.G. (1987), *The Sovereign Entrepreneur: Oil Policies in Advanced and Less Developed Capitalist Countries*, Ithaca: Cornell University Press.

Masters, C.D. et al (1987), *World Resources of Crude Oil, Natural Gas, Natural Bitumen and Shale Oil*, World Petroleum Congress.

Mortimer, R. (1974), *Indonesian Communism Under Sukarno: Ideology and Politics 1959–65*, Ithaca and London: Cornell University Press.

National Development Information Office (NDIO) (1993), *Indonesia: Source Book*, Jakarta: NDIO.

Pertamina (1993), *Serving the People*, Jakarta: Pertamina.

Rickleys, M.C. (1981), *A History of Modern Indonesia*.

Schneider, S.A. (1983), *The Oil Price Revolution*, Baltimore: Johns Hopkins University Press.

Siddayo, C.M. (1980), *National Resources of South East Asia*.

United States Department of Commerce (1977), *Energy Interrelationships: A Handbook of Tables and Conversion Factors for Combining and Comparing International Energy Data*, Washington: IDEA.

Vatikiotis, M.R.J. (1993), *Indonesian Politics Under Suharto: Order, Development and Pressure for Change*, London: Routledge.

World Bank, Industry and Energy Department (1992), *Steam Coal for Power and Industry: Issues and Scenarios*, Energy Series Working Paper No. 58, Washington: World Bank.

World Energy Council (1992), *Survey of Energy Resources*, London: WEC.

# INDEX